What people are saying about Hot Dish Confidential:

"*Hot Dish Confidential* will charm you, make you laugh, and teach you how to cook. It is impossible to resist the story of how apricot jam can lead you to the love of your life."—Lynn Hightower, internationally bestselling author of *The Beautiful Risk*

"*In Hot Dish Confidential*, George Sorensen takes the reader on a wild and hilarious adventure as he learns to be a gourmet cook. He does this by throwing dinners featuring different countries—France, Italy, Germany, to name a few. While the stories can be harrowing at times—baked peaches that should be served fresh, and other cooking disasters—Sorensen gamely continues on his quest. In the end he not only conquers the feast, he romances a lovely fellow chef and their jam takes honors at the state fair. A piece de resistance indeed!"—Mary Logue, author of *The Big Sugar*

"With just a pinch of wisdom, a shake of humor and a heaping helping of good old fashion imagination, George has managed to serve up a mighty meal in this book." Duncan Rouleau Co-Creator of *Big Hero Six* and *Ben 10*

Hot Dish

Confidential

*That Year My Friends
Taught Me to Cook*

By George Sorensen

Flexible Press
Minneapolis, Minnesota, 2024

Print ISBN: 979-8-9887213-4-5
eBook ISBN: 979-8-9887213-5-2

Flexible Press LLC
Minneapolis, Minnesota
www.flexiblepub.com
Editors William E Burleson
Vicki Adang, Mark My Words Editorial Services, LLC
Cover: William E Burleson
Cover illustration: Mark Fearing
Author photo: Bradley Sellers

For my friend Joey Ford
and my classmates from the
Campus Laboratory School class of 1963
in San Diego, California

Contents

September 1
   Dining with the Gastronomically Correct 2
   Great Balls of Wonder Bread 5
   Succulent Stratoscoop Parafoils 8
   The Invincibility of Peach Tarts 11
October 23
   Goddess of Unseasoned Food 24
   A Measure of Greatness 31
   Café-Style Accordion 35
   Tasty Kangaroomerangs 39
November 47
   Blooming in the Gastronomic Desert 48
   Germans Who Think They're French 50
   Death Row 53
   Bottle in a Restaurant 61
   Radio-Free Reggie 63
   Out of the Tent 67
   Eva Strikes Back 70
December 73
   Filberts Roasting on an Open Fire 74
   An Amish Rocket Scientist 80
   All the Right Smells 85
   All-Night Goose 86
   Bubble and Squeak 91
January 93
   A Little Vague on the Details 94
   Antipodal Juxtaposition 97
   Under the Sea 100
   Marinated Man-Eaters 101
   Over to France 105

February 115

   The Observable Universe 116

   Brazil 118

   An Unreliable Form of Conveyance 123

   Two Gentlemen Want to Cook You Dinner 124

March 131

   Let's Do the Mash 132

   Mix Your Mustard Daily 137

April 145

   Pan-Blackened Meals 146

   Don't Mince Words 147

   All Gourmeted Out 154

   Cutting Up in Class 156

May 159

   Stealth Mushrooms 160

   Fruiting Your Media 172

June 181

   Rattlesnake Enchiladas 182

   Longnecks! No Stubbies! 183

July 195

   Metal Fume Fever 196

   Pitching Tent in the Jam Wilderness 203

August 213

   Oort Man the Greek 214

   Jamming 222

   After Dinner 229

Acknowledgments 231

About the Author 232

Hot Dish

Confidential

September

Dining with the Gastronomically Correct

SOME FRIENDS INVITED me over for dinner.

Never knowing quite what to expect, I strolled into their house to find Bjorn in the kitchen wearing a splattered apron and insulated gloves. The rich, pungent smell around him seemed discretely engineered to please his sophisticated palette. On the counter, a substantial piece of meat turned on a small electric spit. Bjorn basted it with a paintbrush. The details of how he could prepare anything like this lay beyond my understanding.

"It's going to be a little while before we eat. Lucretia's upstairs changing," he explained. "And I'm roasting pork using a recipe for wild boar."

I took a big whiff of the spicy aroma and studied the kitchen setup. Colors from the house's white stucco walls and terra-cotta roof were duplicated in the wallpaper and interior trim scheme. Very nice, but nothing about the stove or utensils suggested this to be the home of a couple of master chefs.

"How do you cook something like fake wild boar?" I asked. "Just toss it on the fire?"

"No. I marinated it overnight." Bjorn exaggerated the words to let me know how stupid I must be to think such a thing. "You've got to keep your eye on it all the way through the operation—basting all the time. And you've got to make the sauce to baste it in."

Bjorn did not look like a cook, even in an apron. He was thin and nervous and very outspoken, and his straight blond hair shook like a mop around the lunar shape of his face. Bjorn was also the most fidgety person I've ever met. He was always in motion, one hand pushing hair back and, when he was smoking, his other hand hiding the cigarette behind his back. He was the only friend I've ever had who smokes.

"How do you use a recipe intended for one thing to cook something else?" I asked, deep feelings of culinary inadequacy surging.

Bjorn tossed the basting brush aside. "Oh, geez, Sorensen. Don't you know? You can cook anything with any recipe if you just tweak it a little, you know, just, I mean—" He pushed his hair up again. "I mean, you just have to know how to do it."

"OK, I'm stupid," I admitted. "Nobody in my family knows how to cook. When I visit home now, they're down to eating frozen pancakes. Who knew freezing pancakes would ever become commercially viable? I don't have any experience to draw on. I grew up with an aerosol can of whipped cream rusting in the refrigerator. How was I supposed to learn to cook with those role models?"

"Well, geez, I don't know," Bjorn said, basting.

I could see big flecks of green on the meat. Herbs, I thought, or seaweed, or some other ingredient I had been deprived of learning about because the Boy Scouts didn't use it in their cooking. Once-a-month boyhood scouting weekends at Camp Hual-Cu-Cuish and Mataguay in the Cuyamacas, an hour east of San Diego, gave me a chance to develop some standard cookery skills. The years I invested to become an Eagle Scout afforded me the opportunity to learn to build fires, plan menus for campouts, and satisfy hungry kids with rudimentary knowledge gleaned from the *Boy Scout Handbook* and *Boys' Life* magazine. Reading these publications, I picked up bits and pieces about practical cooking, gained confidence working with basic ingredients under a variety of conditions—rainstorms, buggy tents, smoky fires. More kitchen skills came from my Boy Scout training than anything I witnessed at home.

"You know," I lamely explained, "I've always wanted to be able to do this gourmet stuff—cook as well as you seem to be able to. How can I learn?"

"To cook?" Bjorn sounded surprised.

"Yeah. I haven't a clue how to go about it."

"Just have somebody show you how to do it—that's how I learned. Remember, I grew up on a farm. You think there were a bunch of gourmets out there?" Bjorn basted and sipped coffee and fussed with his hair. "We'll show you how to do it. Maybe we can have some people over."

Cautiously revealing an insecurity about not knowing something it seemed every adult should know, I said, "I've been thinking about doing some sort of a gourmet thing."

"To have people show you?"

"Something more formal than that. Do a series of dinners with different themes—styles from different countries. I could finally learn my way around the kitchen if I put together the right group of people and watched what they do. Why not make an evening out of it?"

"Yeah, well," Bjorn said as juices dripped, "Lucretia and I'll do that with you. She's a great cook. We both are. Sounds like fun."

"If you'll help me out, I'll organize it. I know a lot of people who can cook quite well. I'm just not one of them."

For years, before Bjorn agreed to help, I had been intrigued by the idea of a gourmet cooking group that informally met, showed off their skills, and shared the pleasure of eating together. However, until the moment I witnessed the alchemy changing domestic pork into roast wild boar, I did not think I would be the one to turn the idea into a reality. I had heard of similar groups that gathered to make a run at different types of cooking and reported varying results. A business acquaintance told me about one group that tried to rotate responsibility so one couple would plan and prepare the entire gourmet evening. They'd purchase and cook the dinner, and members would come over to eat. This group disintegrated when its organizers sensibly tried to charge each person $20 to cover the cost. People balked: "We aren't going to pay twenty bucks to come over to eat at somebody's house. We're just going over to their house for heaven's sake."

The same folks who would—without a second thought—spend $100 each for so-so cooking at an overheated restaurant with abhorrent service wouldn't chip in a fraction of that amount to share the gastronomic bonding of personalized, first-class cooking out of a friend's kitchen. A bit shortsighted. Surely pettiness and politics have no place in a gourmet kitchen. I naively thought my gourmet group would be above all that.

That is how the idea got started. After spending more than thirty years staring into the refrigerator, I would devote a year to learning to cook at the hands of well-meaning friends. Everything I did during these months would relate to the pursuit of the pleasures of cooking.

I didn't realize the amount of gastronomic hardship I would face as a result—or that nothing about my life would ever be the same.

Great Balls of Wonder Bread

THE WEEK FOLLOWING my decision to organize these dinners, I tried to dredge up every memory of useful cooking skills I had acquired growing up. A few set routines formed my earliest dining impressions. Every Sunday my parents would get a roast—beef, of course—and roast it without benefit of sauces, seasonings, or ornamentation: 350°F until the glass meat thermometer registered well-done. For the rest of the week, we'd eat leftover beef with thick veins of fat running through it. I heated beef slices in the toaster oven after school, along with balled-up Wonder Bread for snacks.

I grew up a long time ago, and vividly recall the era of eating TV dinners. Frozen meals, with each course segregated by compartments in an aluminum tray, appeared in grocery stores as televisions did in living rooms and were the go-to dinner for a long time. At some point, the Swanson Company enlarged its TV dinners to include soup—with its own lid—and apple cobbler. The foil over the dessert had to be folded back to brown the top of the cobbler. I felt a lot of responsibility to fold it just right. The most vivid memory from these dinners remains the spine-tingling drag of my fork on the aluminum bottom while watching a TV show.

When Bjorn suggested beginning our gourmet group with a Northern Italian theme, I was surprised by how much I looked forward to exploring it, given my introduction to different types of food—Italian cooking in particular.

"You'll love it. Northern Italian is a great starting point," Bjorn said during one of our many conversations on the form the gourmet dinners would take. "Jump into this gourmet thing with both feet. Come on, let's do Northern Italian just to get you started."

My first impressions of Italian and other types of cooking came from my childhood experiences while going out to eat. An Italian restaurant was one of three family-run places we frequented that created their own menus and atmospheres.

Setting an early standard, Ramon's Mexican Restaurant served thick, skin-on fries made from whole potatoes cut lengthwise. I was very taken by their moody painting of an Indian prince and princess blending into a mountain range. It hung over a row of Ramon's booths, and I spent most of the time studying the painting's black velvet depths.

The second dining spot offered American truck-stop cooking. Bob's Coffee Shop had a wall of windows in front and the first plastic-covered menus I had ever held in my eight-year-old hands.

However, an Italian restaurant made the largest impression of all. Near a long-defunct Uni-Mart, this place operated out of a small converted house. A big bright sign on the roof flashed *D'Angelo's Italian Food*. The living room and adjacent porch bore checkered tablecloths and straw-basket Chianti bottles thick with wax from dripping candles.

As we strolled in one night, D'Angelo himself—a short, happy man with a thick five o'clock shadow—greeted my family. He wore a cheap tuxedo and gold cufflinks. His accent intimidated me. On this epic visit, he used broad hand gestures while explaining how to twirl spaghetti. I had been using the stuff-and-bite approach, which involved loading a wad of noodles into my mouth so they looked like a bunch of broken venetian blinds hanging down my chin, then biting off the ends, dropping them back onto the plate.

I didn't care much for spaghetti. The tomato sauce always got on my shirt, no matter how hard I tried to keep it from happening. The meatballs buried beneath the noodles had no flavor. But since it was the only thing on the menu remotely familiar to me, I always ordered it.

Two bites into dinner and D'Angelo leaned over me with a big smile stretched across his cheeks, his eyes like lanterns shining on my young face. "Watch me. This a better way. It be all right, OK?" (He really did talk this way.)

"He'll show you how to do it," my father said, indicating I should pick up my fork and spoon and follow D'Angelo's directions.

My face red from embarrassment and confused by the man's accent, I watched as D'Angelo took my spoon in one hand and twiddled my fork in the other. How badly had I shamed my family that they would do this to me in public?

"You twirl the spaghetti with the fork, hold it in the spoon, so you don't have to bite it off. Like this. Look. See?" D'Angelo plunged the fork through a few strands of spaghetti and spun them into a bite-size ball in the basin of the spoon—a quick little move, all fingertips. "Now you try."

Traumatized like any decent kid, I followed instructions as my sister, mother, father, the entire dining room, and D'Angelo watched. I struggled with the process, speared too many strands, twirled self-consciously, created an orb the size of Gibraltar around my fork, and forced it into my mouth. My lips didn't touch. I could barely chew. I looked like a booming prairie chicken as strands of spaghetti hung between my teeth like escaping worms.

"Oh, good try," D'Angelo said, grinning down at me, talking with his fingers. "If I could just make a suggestion. A little thought. Perhaps. Next time. Twirl just a slightly smaller ball. Just a little suggestion for you."

I did not take another bite of spaghetti for years.

Needing to plan the first gourmet dinner intelligently, I fled to the library and bookstores to discover the arguable differences distinguishing Northern from Southern Italian cooking. Most resources agreed that Italians make white sauces in the North because that region has more milk. The North also uses more rice and polenta—a robust cooked cornmeal—and they raise more beef. Northern Italy is broken into several states, some with familiar names like the Piedmont, Lombardy, and Tuscany. Northerners, it is also said, twirl their pasta in their spoons because they are more cultured.

In the south, Italians thrive on red sauces because of an abundance of tomatoes. And they twirl their pasta on plates because—as a friend who visited relatives there insisted at great length—Southerners are a little less refined. Spaghetti and meatballs, pizza, and lasagna come from the South, and because this poorer region sent countless waves of immigrants to America, these dishes became ubiquitous in the States.

There hasn't always been such a clear-cut north-south division. Before Italy's unification in 1861, each city-state had its own ruler, customs, dialect, cultural peccadilloes, and methods of preparing meals. Many sources described Italian cooking as an elaboration of peasant fare—basically all the best cooking started with ingredients scratched out of local forests. The most sophisticated menu originated from people making do with available ingredients. Gritty peasant food tends to elevate itself over centuries. No exception, Italian cooking improved as the country gained various popes, Caesars, and ranking families who demanded more sophisticated cuisine. With all its influences, Italian cuisine evolved into one of the most popular and flexible cuisines in the world. Any chef with half a wit can interpret it. Few other cooking styles can survive that kind of punishment with their integrity so deliciously intact.

Succulent Stratoscoop Parafoils

I KNEW EVEN though Italians divide their cooking into north and south, Americans do not. Many chefs consider Italian recipes a wide-open opportunity to tinker in the kitchen. As with many things I discovered during a year of gastronomic hardship, this knowledge came in fragments rather than in neat progression. Learning to cook isn't a simple linear event. I learned this and more pointers about Italian cooking as I camped down the Oregon coast, working my way south on an annual pilgrimage to the Shakespeare Festival in Ashland. I pulled into a crowded state campground on the north side of Newport. After pitching my tent, I drove into town.

The persistent wind off the Pacific feels like an invisible wall all summer, and it's wasteful to be on an Oregon beach without a kite. To take care of this, I wandered into the Catch the Wind kite store.

Under the yawning red-and-yellow mouth of a thirty-five-foot lucky dragon, I asked the manager—a wind-burned young woman wearing red shorts and a faded red T-shirt—where the locals went to eat. Without hesitation she tossed a hand off toward the ocean.

"Don Petrie's. You gotta go."

"Italian?"

"Yeah. Don Petrie's Italian Food Company."

"Northern or Southern?"

"Neither—remember, you're in Oregon. It's kind of his own Italian. Petrie Italian. His seafood lasagna is legendary around here, and he sells his sauces by the quart. They're awesome."

I bought a yellow Skynasaur stunt kite and headed out.

Even though I had asked for a local hangout, I expected Don Petrie's Italian Food Company to be more visually aggressive. I drove past it twice because I was looking for a sign with the size and lack of restraint of the McDonald's arches. I didn't notice the understated restaurant that blended into an older residential neighborhood. Petrie's occupied what used to be a mom-and-pop grocery—a square, human-scaled structure left over from an era of tight-knit neighborhoods and personalized service.

The building sat snugly on a corner four blocks from the ocean, across the street from a vacant lot. If the sun hadn't already set, it would have been easier to spot the red, white, and green exterior, and the words *Vino, Minestrone, Lasagna, Seafood, and Dinners* painted across the wooden awning. It wasn't visible in this light. Neither could I at first see the cluster of paper signs taped across the front windows with lettering too small to read from any distance: *Bottomless Baskets of Garlic Bread, Fresh Fish Pasta, Sauces to Go*. I couldn't tell if the restaurant was even open until I parked, walked over, and peeked in. So many people filled the tables it didn't look like there was room for anybody else. However, once I was inside, a woman with thick Mediterranean eyebrows waved a menu and led me around a corner into a larger secret room full of booths and tables and a calmer private atmosphere.

The fog of a thousand garlic cloves, sun-ripened tomatoes, and fresh oregano thickened the air. As I passed the kitchen, I saw the chef standing in the mist: Don Petrie nodded shyly. He appeared to be a peaceful man, well fed, with a linebacker's neck and a serene mustache. He wore a faded T-shirt—like everybody else in Newport.

Petrie's thirty years of experience as a cook started with a stint in the National Guard before he opened the first Italian restaurant on the Oregon coast. He began with simple servings of pizza and á la carte items, and gradually elaborated on his menu to develop four-course dinners. Just like the kite-store manager said, it wasn't Northern or Southern—it was Petrie Italian, which a sample of Petrie's entrées shows:

Last Chicken in Newport
Specially seasoned chicken breast, mushrooms and artichoke hearts blended with creamy Marsala wine sauce. Served over fettuccine.

Red Snapper Marinara
Filet of red snapper baked in a sauce of tomatoes, green peppers, celery, onions and garlic. Covered with Pacific shrimp and white wine. Served with pasta.

Seafood Fettuccine
Green noodles and a light cream sauce with a touch of lemon, topped with sautéed flakes of fresh snapper and lots of Pacific shrimp.

Number Fourteen
Half manicotti with pasta and sauce of your choice from seven sauces in the Sauce Pot. Recommendation: The clam sauce made of onions, garlic, Parmesan cheese and lots of clams. Thickened with a butter roux. Additional sauce choices: Don's meat, Don's vegetarian, spicy sausage, marinara, lemon cream or Parmesan cheese sauce.

I chose the baked seafood lasagna: a deep dish of layered scallops, Pacific shrimp, lingcod, and red snapper, together with lasagna noodles and broccoli, olives, mozzarella, provolone, and Parmesan cheeses. It was baked in a rich lemon cream sauce that oozed through the strata of pasta. It took two hours to eat. It redefined my understanding of what might come out of the Italian kitchen.

The Invincibility of Peach Tarts

MANY ACQUAINTANCES HAD mentioned to me they possessed a knowledge of upscale cooking, so I started to make a list of possible participants for the Northern Italian dinner. I called a number of people to ask if they were interested, and to those who were, I sent out an informal announcement about this first gourmet event. I expected a slow response, but my phone started ringing with questions about all this. Everyone was willing to cook major entrées, salads, breads, desserts, or whatever was needed to round out the meal. I only needed to pick and choose from the offerings to create the menu.

This showed promise, though the momentum intimidated me because I still had to prepare something myself. To play it safe, I wanted to cook a relatively simple dish that could not fail.

"Try a dessert, Sorensen," Bjorn advised. "You can't screw that up too bad. A lot of people don't eat desserts anyway, so it won't matter so much if you blow it."

"Thanks for your confidence," I said with the thought that a dessert would be all right if it had several stages in its production. That way I wouldn't have to stretch creating it. I scanned a hundred cookbooks for my heroic debut and found a novice-friendly peach tart with Northern Italian written all over it.

No sooner had I announced the menu and decided what I would cook than it seemed like the designated Saturday had arrived. I started on the dessert project early in the day. When my fellow gourmets arrived, I would already be done and could learn about their techniques. At the grocery store, I handpicked the best and biggest fresh peaches. They looked luminous, a brilliant Northern Italian deep yellow-orange bursting with fresh flavor. I selected the best all-purpose flour and found myself pushing a cart through the gourmet food section, disappointed the list wasn't any longer and I couldn't make more of the whole process.

Back at the house, I set up the kitchen the way a surgeon organizes an operating room. My meager collection of bowls, knives, and towels laid in rows. I arranged the groceries on the counter in the order they would be used. Then I created the syrup and made the dough for the crust, pressing it into little individual pans. I peeled the peaches by first dipping them in hot water to loosen the skins. I sliced and placed the peaches in the doughy crusts, poured syrup over them, and slid the tarts into the preheated oven.

I casually glanced back through the recipe. What had I missed? Anything? Impossible. I experienced a moment of contentment before something snagged my mind. How closely had I followed that recipe? Had I gotten distracted and put it together too fast?

The tarts sat in the oven for one hot minute. I paced the kitchen, wondering if I had read the directions right. What had they said? A second hot minute. A fresh peach tart goes into the oven? How long could you bake peaches and keep them fresh? Hold on! I threw open the cookbook and pored over the recipe, retracing the steps. Maybe I hadn't actually read all the way through the instructions as thoroughly as I should have. Is it possible not to have picked up the intent of the author? A surge of panic.

My bare hands grabbed the oven door, flung it down. Heat mushroomed into my face. I yanked the baking sheet in one dramatic swoop, and the tarts slid all over. Fortunately, they weren't much above room temperature, and the peaches showed no obvious signs of shriveling. I recouped. The poorly written, fresh peach tart recipe explained the empty crusts were to be baked and cooled, then the peaches and syrup placed in them.

I disassembled the tarts, this time carefully following the recipe.

Even though the tarts turned out perfectly, I beat myself up over the mistake and became angry about not understanding the recipe. As I began reading more cookbooks, the differences between the ways recipes are written became more evident. This turned into a major gastronomic lesson. Some recipe authors are very straightforward, providing little more than the ingredients listed like carburetor parts. Others create cookbooks of flowing prose that translate easily to the kitchen.

Ascending the first step on the gastronomic learning curve, I discovered that recipes are not holy scriptures. They can be poorly organized, ingredients can be left out, and incorrect temperatures and cooking times can be given. Recipes can be as draggy and boring as bad novels, or as tense and theatrical as a best-selling thriller. Recipes are too often written by experts overly involved in cooking every day. What these people turn out of the kitchen may be fantastic, but when they write down a recipe, they can't communicate what they know. Developing the ability to criticize cookbooks and differentiate between a well-written recipe and a hack job turned into a major lesson.

Really good recipes—I found out—introduce you to a dish as if it were an old friend. They take you along, leading you on a tour of an exotic, aromatic land where every twist and turn is magic.

Things began to move quickly in the few hours before the gourmets arrived at my place. I started to bustle around, worried my place wouldn't be adequate for picky cooks.

And I had reason to worry. My house didn't amount to much. Built in 1908, the second floor was one of those half-sized jobs where the walls only come up to your waist before the roof slants in. The whole place couldn't have been bigger than about 800 square feet. With my arms spread, I could practically touch both sides of the living room. The kitchen, the place to which people gravitate when they come over, had been extended when I knocked out a wall.

One major problem with entertaining in my house seemed increasingly critical as the time for guests to arrive drew nearer: I did not own a table and chairs. In the past, when friends stopped by, we sat on my couch, which was just wide enough for two people to squeeze onto. In the event more showed up, I had four bright yellow metal folding chairs. An extra person could always sit on the rattan coffee table, and if that wasn't enough, they could plunk down on my old stereo speakers.

I figured there would be places to sit since Bjorn and Lucretia were bringing more folding chairs. The gourmets would just have to hold their plates in their laps, picnic-style. Not very sophisticated, even if I hadn't begun my freelance writing career all that long ago and there wasn't a lot of cash available to throw at indulgences like furniture. But, oddly enough, things worked out. About noon, a garage sale sign went up in front of a dilapidated house down the block. Inside the basement, thirty tables, a dozen highboys with peeling veneer, and other broken-down items from foreclosure properties had been consolidated. I negotiated the asking price to $16 for a table with swooping Queen Anne legs and got help carrying it home.

I covered the stained tabletop with my one worn tablecloth, rubbed the spots off my easily bent flatware, and put out the plates. I put on my apron: silk-screened with a picture of Alfred Hitchcock. But when a lanky artist buddy of mine stopped by and told me it made me look fat, I quickly took it off.

Early on in the planning process, Bjorn and I decided it best to establish a core group of enthusiasts as the foundation of these dinners. This central group would always be invited, but to keep things from going stale, I told Bjorn, "I'll ask for suggestions about people to invite every now and then—some friends who could add to the occasion, teach me something about cooking, and not be concerned that they were only invited sporadically."

"Yeah, OK. Call them alternates," Bjorn said, letting it go at that.

I had just finished getting the house ready when a pair of alternates arrived. Babs, a fragile-looking woman with a Barbie doll figure and porcelain complexion, spoke softly about her job in hospital administration. Her husband, Ricardo, bewildered and gaunt, wore a sooty tweed jacket, smoked a pipe, and said he was in marketing. I had not met them before, and when they appeared, I experienced an uncomfortable sense that these people had just returned from an alien abduction.

A weird nervousness set in. Was this the experience I really wanted? Were these the people I wanted it with? A gourmet dinner suddenly seemed a dangerous proposition. As more people arrived, I expected it to start looking like a Fellini film. I wasn't sure how to handle things. What social skills did I have? I hadn't done much formal entertaining, so I fell back on the memories of how my family handled dinner parties. I recalled my father who coped by putting the emphasis on alcohol and giving his guests great big drinks.

To stock his bar, he kept a set of liquor bottles from top-shelf brands. These were empty, and before the guests arrived, he'd get a funnel and fill the expensive bottles with cheap gin, bourbon, rum, and vodka. When I questioned this maneuver, even asked if it wasn't cheating, he explained it away: "I see no reason to pay that kind of money for a bunch of other people to drink my expensive liquor. They can't tell the difference." No wonder so many of his guests went home complaining of headaches.

Already these amateur gourmet events were unlocking my early experiences with food and drink. It surprises me which details I remember about childhood events that later reveal hidden messages. One was noise. I recall ice clinking around in cocktail glasses as the predominant sound at family gatherings. Lots of people standing around, the smell of cooking from the kitchen, but no talk about food, just the sound of ice clinking around in the drinks. This recollection helps me better guess why in America there is so much knowledge about mixing drinks and so little about decent cooking.

Everywhere you go, coast to coast, in the smallest towns in the most out-of-the-way spots, there will be a bartender who knows how to make a decent martini. Try to find a great chef in the same town—chances are there aren't any. In Europe, it's the other way around. You have to scour the countryside for a tolerable mixed drink, if you can even find one, while great chefs are tripping all over one another in the tiniest, most out-of-the-way hamlets.

So as Babs and Ricardo strolled into the kitchen, I nervously offered them, by reflex, a drink. "Would you like a Bombay martini to get started?"

"Yes. Yes," the Barbie wife said.

"Yes, I'd like that," her husband nodded, obviously considering it a treat.

I broke out my Bombay gin: a tall, slim bottle with the confident picture of Queen Victoria in cameo at the top of the label. I poured the real expensive stuff, none of that bottle switching. The ritual of offering a drink to guests is something I had learned exhibited adult behavior. Didn't it?

As good as I felt playing nervous bartender at that moment, my heart sank when I realized this couple had been assigned to bring wine for the evening. Taking the luscious martinis, I had poured them, Babs and Ricardo placed two rather ordinary, inexpensive wine bottles on the kitchen island. The liquid in them looked slightly blue in the overhead light. I didn't recognize the name of the vineyard or the country it was from. Perhaps it was from Mars or some distant vineyard in the Milky Way. I thought the people assigned to the wine might bring a case. Or barring that expense, they would at least cheap out and show up with jug wine—we needed volume.

Naturally, once the dozen or so people arrived, they went through the two bottles of wine very quickly. Then they downed my whole bottle of gin. I sped over to a nearby store and purchased a very large bottle of Bardolino—a Northern Italian wine in a bottle the size and shape of a scuba tank—and they drank all that too. Ricardo wandered the house, filling up glasses without asking people if they wanted more, as if he'd brought the wine himself.

Most everyone who brought food finished preparing it once they arrived. At first this amounted to chaos, with so many people competing for oven space and room on the stove. Things settled down quickly, and I learned a great deal about assembling raw ingredients and reducing sauces—basics I knew nothing about. I could ask questions and help wherever needed, so it became as valuable an experience as I had hoped.

After they finished cooking, Bjorn and Lucretia threaded their way through the gathering, smiling, introducing themselves to people they didn't know. Lucretia had an egghead job with a manufacturer. She traveled all the time, drowned herself in meetings, and dressed the part of a fast-rising executive. Taller than her husband, perky, and alert, Lucretia never wore the same outfit twice. She didn't even appear to mix and match. Everything looked like an outfit she'd just taken out of the wrapper. That evening she wore a flowered sundress and shiny sandals, and had fixed her hair up in curls.

While Bjorn and Lucretia were well prepared, two other core members of the group—the Dutes—weren't. I had met Bob Dute when I got tangled up in a tricky mortgage. He was the first loan officer I found at any bank who was more interested in the people sitting across the desk from him than in the dowdy bunch of forms he filled out each day. I sensed he knew the tacit threat of the bank's power to take away your house, car, and all your possessions, and completely ruin your life was intimidation enough without his having to be obvious about it.

Bob's wife often traveled out of town on business or to visit her relatives, so when I was getting to know Bob, he'd come over on his own. He had an interest in upscale eating and drinking, and spoke of his Coast Guard days on the Olympic Peninsula when the guardsmen would boil mountains of crabs in steel drums. Each time Bob told the story, details about approaching storms, size of the surf, and the language of the fishermen took on a more heroic character. When I suggested the gourmet dinner concept to him, he was enthusiastic, and I got word back that his wife was too. I knew the Dutes would help in my gourmet education.

When the Dutes strolled into the packed kitchen, apprehension about the unfamiliar situation wrinkled their faces. I introduced them to the group. "This is Bob." He smiled, looking around the room. I had seen him wearing a suit at the bank so often that he looked quaint wearing yellow shorts and a shirt. As his wife walked through the doorway behind him, my mind blanked. She smiled beautifully, flawless white teeth sparkling, her blond hair pulled back gracefully, framing peach-like pink cheeks. She'd kept her maiden name, and easygoing about other things, she was very particular about it.

"This is Bob Dute and—" for an instant I couldn't remember exactly what his wife said she wanted to be called, "and this is...Mrs. Dute."

Everyone froze as I braced myself for how my mistaken would be taken. Fortunately for me, she just laughed and smiled, and she's been Mrs. Dute to everyone since.

Bob and Mrs. Dute were totally unprepared for the Northern Italian dinner. They greatly underestimated the number of people who would come, seriously misunderstood how gastronomically intense we intended to get, and brought only one pint of Italian ice. Not enough for twelve gourmets. Hardly enough for two.

"We're so embarrassed," Bob said, motioning for Ricardo to refill his wine glass. "I don't know what we were thinking. Next time we'll do it right."

Mrs. Dute gave an embarrassed giggle. "We just didn't realize people were going to be so, well, you know—so hungry." She hailed from South Dakota, a state not unfamiliar with ample helpings, but I supposed we were all on a learning curve.

"Don't worry about it," I told the Dutes as I dug into the refrigerator. I used a tiny scoop to gouge cantaloupe balls and place them in small dishes. Combining the cantaloupe with dabs of their Italian ice would stretch out the servings and make them decorative enough to pass.

Aside from the shortages, which I figured resulted from my inexperience organizing the event, everything went nicely. The dining experience exceeded any I had had in my house, partly because of the energy put into the food preparation itself and the intensity of the participants. The rest seemed to come with the knowledge that something good was beginning to happen in my kitchen. I learned to make fresh penne with white sauce. Ricotta, onion, and parsley frittata. Zucchini salad. Baked polenta with Bolognese Parmesan sauce. Sweet-and-sour onions, peas, and prosciutto.

One recipe stood out from the others: the Lombardy Veal Rolls in Tomato Sauce.

A word about recipes.

It is good to share an occasional recipe with friends. I will start with this one. I see recipes as part of the gastronomic narrative and don't write all of my recipes in all the same way. They don't follow a set format or consistently include a separate list of ingredients. This is part of their charm.

When headed to the grocery store, I print out the whole recipe and take it along. Some cooks prefer one list with all the ingredients, while

I prefer the entire recipe on a piece of paper scrunched up my pocket. It's exciting when finding everything you need to cook dinner becomes a treasure hunt.

Ingredients get crossed off the recipe as I make my way around the store and they find their way into my shopping cart. This method helps me better understand how a recipe works, plus it feels more organic to the cooking process than shopping from a simple list.

Recipes can be written in different ways, so make sure to read the whole thing through many times before shopping or cooking, to make sure you have everything you need and understand what steps are involved in preparation. If you like to shop from an ingredient list and don't have one, then take a minute to write one out before you head to the store.

Lombardy Veal Rolls in Tomato Sauce

Serves 6 or more

Make the stuffing

- ✓ ¼ pound finely chopped prosciutto
- ✓ 1 cup chopped fresh spinach
- ✓ 2 tablespoons chopped parsley
- ✓ 2 eggs
- ✓ 2 teaspoons heavy cream
- ✓ 1 teaspoon dried oregano
- ✓ 1 teaspoon dried basil
- ✓ 2 tablespoons seasoned breadcrumbs
- ✓ ½ cup grated Parmesan cheese
- ✓ ½ teaspoon grated nutmeg
- ✓ 2 whole cloves, smashed
- ✓ Dash pepper

To prepare the stuffing: Add above ingredients to a food processor and pulse until well mixed, or mix in a bowl with a wooden spoon.

Lightly pound out 12 slices veal scaloppini to about 4 x 6 inches. Place 1 to 1½ tablespoons stuffing on each veal slice. Roll and tie with string to secure.

To brown the veal rolls: In a large sauté pan, combine 2 tablespoons butter and 2 tablespoons olive oil. Heat over medium flame until butter mixture bubbles. Add veal rolls and cook 2 to 3 minutes, turning as needed to brown on all sides. Remove rolls from pan and set aside.

Make the sauce

- ✓ 1 chopped medium onion
- ✓ 2 minced cloves garlic
- ✓ 2 tablespoons olive oil
- ✓ 1 cup white wine

Place the above ingredients in the pan. Heat over medium flame for 5 minutes, stirring and scraping what's left of the veal rolls from the bottom.

Add

- ✓ 2 16-ounce cans tomato sauce
- ✓ 1 tablespoon dried basil
- ✓ A dash of black pepper

Stir over medium heat for 5 minutes. Add veal rolls and continue to cook, turning rolls and stirring sauce until rolls are heated through and sauce thickens. Pour sauce over rolls to serve.

Dried herbs should be crushed to release their flavor.

Like so many of the best recipes, this one came from one of the primary participants in the group, a mountaineer named Jay Berne. Pronounced "Bur-knee."

October

Goddess of Unseasoned Food

JAY CAME OVER to me at the end of the first dinner, eyes twinkling. "Now that we've done Northern Italy, George, what do you want to do? The South of France? Oh, wait, let me think about this. You're going to use up all the good food there is at this rate. Why don't we do some bad theme in between Northern Italian and the South of France? Stick in some toasted iguana from Guatemala or something from the restaurants I went to in Mexico—places with a dirt floor and a dog under the table. That'd make you look forward to the South of France."

When Jay Berne talked food, I listened. His exploits in the kitchen had grown into legends passed among friends. He'd taken classes at a French-run cooking school at the Sofitel Hotel chain and occasionally won recipe contests. No cooking terms were foreign to him. Ask about cooking an exotic meatloaf? He knew something about it. Couldn't figure out how to debone a strange fish? Call Jay. He enjoyed taking his time in the kitchen, relishing each step as he moved methodically through a recipe, using the most studied approach of anyone I had watched cook.

Jay was not particularly tall. Though, he was one of those compact people who didn't seem all that small. His shaggy mane and beard started to turn white when he was still in high school. He managed a large camping equipment store, so no matter the occasion, he reliably wore camping clothes—gray-flecked wool socks, Patagonia polo shirts, and low-top walking shoes with Vibram soles—lending a scent of pine needles and a snapping breeze to all that surrounded him.

I thought about his suggestion of the South of France. "You don't think we should just go for the best? French cooking is supposed to be it."

"Are you gonna pace yourself?"

What did I know? Maybe we *should* break up the more celebrated food with lesser-known cuisine. Considering this, I told Jay something I remembered about the first time I visited France. I was sixteen years old, traveling with my parents. We never made it to the south, though I have a vivid recollection of watching Paris traffic, which at that time was much more a mixture of bicycles and scooters than it is today. There weren't so many big cars and buses. Pedestrians had more of a run of the place.

I stood on a corner as a man, pants legs rolled, came pedaling his bicycle. On the back rack were two long, thin loaves of bread—classic baguettes, adding charm to the picture of a busy Paris street.

The man looked good, but unfortunately cycled poorly. He pedaled along, ignoring crosswalk lines, pushing through a crowd trying to make its way across the street. His bicycle intercepted a middle-aged gentleman wearing a red beret. Instead of stopping, or even slowing down to let the man pass, the cyclist stood up on the pedals and rammed his bicycle through. The beret flew off, the pedestrian stumbled, then lit out after the cyclist, catching up with him in a few steps. He yanked the bread out of the bike rack and broke both baguettes across his knee.

The cyclist screeched to a stop, his face a twisted mask of horrified disbelief as the pedestrian shoved the halves of the broken loaves into the cyclist's arms and proudly walked away.

Jay rolled his eyes. "You see what happened, don't you? The guy who got knocked down did the worst thing he possibly could do to the bicyclist. It's the harshest penalty one Frenchman can dish out to another. He ruined his dinner."

Wondering about the French's preoccupation with exceptional food and initiating my own gourmet dinner group led me to reexamine the everyday cooking techniques typical to my friends. In America, the best cooking a family has to offer is summoned three times a year: The Holidays, gastronomic shorthand for Easter, Thanksgiving, and Christmas—or substitute Passover, Hanukkah, the summer solstice, pagan and patriotic celebrations, annual picnics, reunions, or your own set of occasions. Most people seem to have three major holidays to contend with each year. These are the principal opportunities to showcase cooking rituals blindly passed down for generations, from grandparent to parent to child. In most homes, when families gather during The Holidays, a regimented set of events takes place. The difficulty with these rituals is they've lost any connection with their origins, and the result is lousy cooking.

To engage in these rituals, a family sits around one long dinner table with the food laid down the center. Conversation is stilted because there is always an old aunt who someone fears offending at some point in the conversation. The distances between people along the endless table are too great, and the angles too bad, for talking to anyone except the person sitting next to you—probably the individual with whom you least wished to converse.

The food is supposedly some of the best you've had all year. How can anybody learn to cook with this kind of example? Would you ever eat this stuff any other time?

Cooking during The Holidays is identical in many ways to a stage play. It's similar to what exuberant Royal Shakespeare Company Director Peter Brook describes as a type of performance he calls Deadly Theatre. In his book, *The Empty Space*, Brook explains that Deadly Theatre is produced when actors are so far removed from their source material, they've lost any tie to its origins. Their performance lacks any understanding of the original motivations of the characters or the significant themes.

Brook uses the example of performances by two Chinese opera companies, one which comes from the mainland and the other from the island of Taiwan. The mainland actors were in touch with their spiritual roots and could draw from the original sources to refresh their memories of the ancient material. They understood what nuances to bring forth and the essence of what they were trying to express. The Taiwanese company—even though it used the same text and had more money for sets and costumes—gave a flat performance, blandly imitating the movements and voicing, lacking a knowledge of the underlying meaning.

Deadly Theatre came to my house during The Holidays, always following the same unwritten script. The dinner ritual began with moving the couch to make room for extra leaves in the table, expanding it to full-blown, aircraft-carrier-deck length. An heirloom box of silverware appeared from the bottom of a closet, requiring arduous polishing after eons of neglect. I remember facing down an endless pile of blackened silverware and a dried-out paste that I thought might be poisonous.

Seldom-seen members of our family arrived like actors checking in with the stage manager before a performance. They took their customary places around the table, and soon big steaming pots of food came in from the kitchen and were passed around. The same menu items were served every time: mashed potatoes, gravy, three kinds of meat—slightly burned spareribs, turkey, and ham. Frozen peas or canned string beans were boiled for hours. A leaf of lettuce beneath a mound of cottage cheese topped with a pineapple ring decorated a small plate. Stiff store-bought pies finished out the meal.

When I asked why we always prepared these things, I got the same answer every time. "It's a family tradition. This is what our family's always had ever since we came from the Old Country."

"But some branches of the family have been in America since before the Revolution. Haven't we had the chance to develop our own American cooking after over two hundred years in the New World?"

"No," came the answer. "Our family's cooking grew out of our Scandinavian roots."

This food's from Scandinavia? You're kidding, I thought. Descendants of the Vikings are supposed to be eating pineapple-topped cottage cheese? I doubt it. All that meat, mashed potatoes, and gravy are Midwestern farm foods.

To be sure, I checked a few authoritative sources on Swedish, Danish, and Norwegian cooking. Reading a purportedly authentic Norwegian cookbook was a stroll through *The Little Shop of Horrors*. Delicacies in Norway include mutton and cabbage, meat cakes, boiled cauliflower, potato rolls, coffee bread, and—hold your breath—cabbage pudding. Even if any of this sounded appetizing in the first place, something had been lost in the translation of Norway's finest cooking as it leapfrogged a couple generations—and several thousand miles—to our table. The recipes had been distorted by distance from the source materials, just as with Brook's Deadly Theatre.

To make a basic change in the way I cooked meant altering my fundamental understanding of the raw materials. The more I worked on what we decided would be the South of France gourmet dinner, the greater the interest I developed in the components. Luckily, I discovered a nearby source I could go to for learning the basics. I went to the fence flanking my backyard.

I discovered one of the best casual cooking authorities in town lived next door. When I moved into my house, the most obvious, and loudest, feature of the neighbors was their dog, a nearsighted boxer with a lot of loyalty to the previous owners of my house. After I moved in, Sir Lancelot spent the first three days barking at two pink plastic flamingos I had stuck out back. On the third day, at precisely 2:32 p.m., the dog grew too hoarse to continue yelping and retreated under an aluminum lounge chair. An hour later the doorbell rang, and a vast woman wearing a tropical coral-colored dress appeared, the exhausted boxer on a nylon leash in one hand, a fresh-baked loaf of yellow-brown crusted bread in the other.

"Hello, neighbor, I'm Eva, and this is Lance," she said cheerfully. "That's short for Sir Lancelot. He's a purebred. Once he gets to know you, he won't bark anymore. Boxers can't see very well, so they go by smells and sounds. He'll get used to your smell real soon."

I introduced myself as she handed over the loaf.

"This is jalapeño bread, just out of the oven," Eva said.

I examined its nectarine color. Little jalapeños poked out around the crust, which smelled warm and rich. The boxer looked up at me, thinking I smelled like bread, I assumed.

"Eva, you do a lot of cooking? Baking?"

"Oh yes, all the time. I enter lotsa contests." She had so much friendly enthusiasm in her voice that I wondered how she could sustain it.

It turned out Eva didn't just bake. She'd won a slew of cooking competitions, bakeoffs, and recipe contests. Ribbons and awards hung all over her kitchen. Eva also grew an herb garden next to the fence dividing our backyards. As I got to know her, we chatted across the fence, and I became interested in what she was growing. When she worked in her garden, I would lean on the white pickets and ask questions about cooking with herbs and spices.

Eva's herb garden looked like a patch of wild prairie crammed into a tiny strip the size and shape of a diving board along the fence. When I finally found out what grew in her garden, the diversity surprised me. Many of the herbs I had not heard of before—certainly not the variations.

Across the fence, I asked, "How do you know what's a weed in what you've got growing there?"

"Sometimes I'm not sure what I've got," she said, standing barefoot in the middle of the herbs.

"How do you know how to use these?"

"Oh, George, it's just cooking with them. You know, follow the recipes and eventually you learn what's best."

I looked to Eva's perpetually cheerful face. "OK, then. What is all this?"

She leaned down, and rooting around with one hand, she separated different strands of green and tore off the top of a spindly plant that had made its way through the herb canopy. She handed it to me. "Smell this—it's lemon thyme. I also have French thyme here, if I can find any." She pulled aside a tall bunch of chives and pointed to a clump beside it. "These are garlic chives. They taste a lot like garlic, but give you a lighter garlic flavor."

Eva continued picking through what looked like grasses, explaining what she had growing in the thick tangle, the tallest strands of which reached her knees. I felt like I was watching Gulliver pick through a Lilliputian jungle. She showed me French tarragon and rosemary. There were three kinds of basil—lemon, sweet, and licorice. Italian marjoram came up beside the fence. Eva explained how she used it in stuffings, with eggplant, and in Greek dishes. And she grew oregano, which she used "on everything and anything really—pizzas and Mexican cooking."

She also had winter and summer savory and two flavors of sage—garden and pineapple. The pineapple sage really did smell like pineapple when she crushed it. Her white-and-green ornamental cabbage was used primarily for garnishing. Sorrel was planted especially for salads. "It's got a deeper, more sour flavor than spinach," she explained. "Sorrel soup is real good, but you have to make sure you follow a decent recipe the first time you make it."

Eva grew fennel, which she braised or used in salad or split under a leg of lamb to add a delicate flavor on the grill. She showed me apple mint, orange mint, spearmint, and plain old regular mint. Parsley, both regular and Italian. Chervil. Shallots. Tomatillos—annual green tomatoes used in salads and Mexican sauces. Bush beans—little beans with no strings when harvested early and with strings when harvested later.

Eva held a little bunch in her hand, "And I also plant little packets of garden mix. These are good when you just need a little something to add in somewhere. I love coming out here, picking through the leaves, trying to figure it all out. It's not really just an herb garden, it's an everything garden."

When it came to leaning over the fence and using some of her herbs, I didn't steal much more than chives, even though she told me I could have whatever I wanted. I just didn't know enough to put them to good use at the time. The better I got to know Eva and her husband, Jim, the more I picked up about cooking. They were always good for a quick insight into a kitchen technique. Jim prided himself on barbecuing, and his extensive travels gave him discerning judgment about restaurants. It was nice to be able to go into the backyard and receive first-class cooking advice.

Another good thing about it: The more time I spent chatting with them across the fence, the less Sir Lancelot barked at me.

A Measure of Greatness

THE MORE I got into my research on the next dinner, the more often I encountered the view that the South of France has the best cooking on earth. The incentive for this greatness must be that the French expect something special whenever they sit down to eat. It also helps that they live in a region where just about anything can grow—fresh herbs, nuts, mushrooms, olives, berries, figs, earthy truffles in exotic variations. They have practically anything anyone would care to eat, and many things that one might not, such as snails, sea urchins, foxes, anchovies, and bunny rabbits.

The South of France punches up its appetites with festivals, particularly saints' days. These are celebrated in spring and summer, creating opportunities for chefs to outperform one another before a critical public. The attractive region varies in color and texture. The coast displays apricot pastels, while protected areas inland are required by law to maintain their original stonework buildings. The beauty runs from rocky hills to abundant woods to lush farmlands to sumptuous vegetation with eucalyptus, palm, and cypress.

Jay Berne prepped me for the South of France dinner over a midweek salad bar lunch. I'd pulled him away from selling post-modern Moss tents to talk about the next gourmet dinner. It was cool out, but Jay wore his shorts and usual sport shirt.

"French cooking," Jay said resolutely, redirecting a lock of shaggy white hair out of his eye. "People make an awful lot out of it. More than they need to. Ask any French chef, they will tell you there are only two techniques to proper cooking. The first is sautéing in oil, which is quick and decisive. The second is slow simmering over a low flame. You can get the hang of those two, can't you? Is it the best cooking on earth? Who can say?"

"I like the idea of choosing between fast and slow cooking," I said, knowing it wasn't that easy but appreciating the simplicity of Jay's breakdown.

He bit into a cherry tomato, and it exploded in his mouth as he said, "The first thing you're going to want to do to prepare authentically for the South of France dinner is to go shopping. Plan to spend hours looking over the vegetables, poking your fingers down into them. Go to several stores and reject almost everything on display. Complain to the clerks. The French, the Italians, most people living in that part of Europe spend a lot of time picking out just the right stuff and complaining. Rejecting almost everything, they check to see how soft the stem of the artichoke feels, search for bruises on the mangos. They're always looking for that perfect ingredient for their recipe. Your South of France dinner needs a long, slow, detailed day of shopping, just to put you in the mood. Then you've got to think about execution of the appropriate technique."

"I feel like I should practice sautéing and simmering."

"Don't practice cooking the way you hit golf balls at a driving range. Cook when you're hungry, and push yourself to try new things. Eventually you're going to want to try the ultimate in French cooking."

Sweat beaded on my brow. "There's an ultimate?"

"Some people wouldn't agree, but people don't always agree to much about cooking. I think figuring out a soufflé includes enough knowledge of physics and chaos theory to make it the ultimate challenge."

Jay provided especially useful tidbits during these lunch meetings. On his advice, I did some quickie practice dishes, using the fast sauté and slow simmer techniques. Finally, I thought I had moved into a new realm of consciousness when I decided that nothing would initiate me into French cooking more thoroughly than mastering a soufflé. Having this arrow in my quiver of recipes seemed like a basic. However, if sautéing and simmering are simple tricks, consistently baking a successful soufflé is witchcraft.

The first five soufflés I took a run at came out looking like tough yellow pancakes baked into the bottom of a shoebox. This changed once I watched an easy soufflé made on the spot for the South of France dinner. I've used the recipe many times since, and it has never failed. Although there is no guarantee with any soufflé, this is as foolproof as it gets.

I cooked the No-Trick Soufflé au Fromage for my parents on the rare occasion of one of their visits, as a special treat they would appreciate. I arose early and arduously prepared it step by step. The soufflé rose beautifully, expanding like a balloon all the way to the roof of the oven, billowing into a brilliant tan. The smell moved sweetly through the house. I'd carefully timed it to finish the instant Mom and Dad came down for breakfast.

"How about a soufflé this morning?"

"I want eggs for breakfast," my father grumbled, stumbling down the stairs. "Scrambled."

"You're having a soufflé." I encouraged his curiosity.

"What's in it?"

"Eggs. You'll like it."

"Eggs," he said suspiciously and slowly took a bite without comment, the way a panther picks at something thrown into its cage.

This soufflé recipe has been part of my kitchen artillery ever since.

No-Trick Soufflé au Fromage

Serves 6

- ✓ ⅓ cup unsalted butter

- ✓ ⅓ cup all-purpose flour

- ✓ 1¾ cups milk

- ✓ ¼ teaspoon white pepper (white pepper won't show)

- ✓ Dash of ground nutmeg

- ✓ 1½ cups shredded Swiss cheese

- ✓ 6 large eggs, slightly beaten with a fork. Don't whack these eggs around too much; they only have to be stirred a little bit, which is one of the distinctive features of this recipe.

Butter and flour a 5- to 6-cup soufflé dish and chill in refrigerator. Melt butter in a medium saucepan, stir in the flour, pepper, and nutmeg. Cook, stirring with a whisk, for one minute. Add milk, bring to a boil, stirring as it thickens. Allow to cook for a few seconds, then remove from heat. Add cheese and mix well with the whisk until melted. Let cool a few minutes, then mix in the eggs.

Pour the mixture into the prepared dish and set aside on the counter for 40 to 45 minutes. Bake at 375° for 50 to 60 minutes, until the top of the soufflé is deep brown and an inserted knife comes out quite dry.

Café-Style Accordion

BJORN ASSIGNED HIMSELF the duty of bringing music to each gourmet gathering. He had access to a warehouse of recordings, so he easily came up with appropriate themes. For the South of France dinner, he played a medley of obscure café accordion tunes with a jaunty air. There are very few things I would describe as jaunty, but that is about the only term you can use for the kind of outdoor café sounds you expect to hear sitting in a sunny sidewalk bistro in Cannes—or for the title music for an early Audrey Hepburn film.

It surprised me that it is actually possible to enjoy listening to the accordion. It is like discovering it's fun to watch bowling. Revelation piled upon revelation throughout my gastronomic experience.

With Bjorn's mood music, the core participants and alternates settled in as one big, happy group. Unlike the first dinner when I jumped for the liquor cabinet, worried people wouldn't be happy without a cocktail in their grip, I didn't feel the need to micromanage everyone's experience quite so much. I consciously decided instead to let the gourmets be responsible for themselves. It helped that these individuals, most of whom had never shared their interest in gourmet cooking with anyone, were quickly getting used to each other, falling into a routine, and establishing a set of tacitly agreed-to, self-managed standards. I never heard anyone spell out exactly what they expected. Everyone just knew they had to cook at an elevated level and freely share information about what they prepared.

The South of France theme made for an interesting evening. For starters, we served an appetizer of salmon-studded scallop mousse with green mayonnaise, followed by Roquefort cream and walnuts in puff pastry. Moving into dinner, I observed the creation of a vegetable dish: gratin of cauliflower with goat cheese and Fontina, which suffered recriminations for not being indigenous to the South of France. For one of the entrées, a sauce crème à la moutarde—a cream-and-mustard sauce—was served in addition to filet de bœuf rôti avec sauce périgueux. This is roast tenderloin of beef with a brown Madeira sauce with truffles. The périgueux must have truffles, so Bob Dute—the chef on this—found some canned truffles that made him suspicious. He backed that up with the mustard sauce. Both sauces were served on the side in case the canned truffles didn't work or people wanted to sample them first.

One of the desserts, a Provençal version of beignets viennois, came off a little thick and sweet. It was made by Rex and his wife, Charlene, an appealing pair who started strong with the group. They jumped at the gourmet dinner idea when I first mentioned it and seemed to like the chance to show off. They were a mystery though. Nobody knew what Rex did for a living, but he seemed to get the bills paid without having an identifiable job.

However he spent his time, Rex looked happy enough. He was neatly groomed too. His hair always looked freshly cut, giving him an air of cleanliness without sharpening his image. A reason for this was he got what looked like three-dollar haircuts. Getting a cheap haircut once a week made his hair look frozen, like it never actually grew.

His longtime live-in-girlfriend-turned-wife took community college classes with the goal of becoming a nursing assistant. Charlene usually had her blood pressure cuff in their living room so she could practice on visitors. Rex openly aired his impatience with Charlene for taking two extra years to get through the training program. It seemed to him she wasn't determined to get any actual work in the field and would be taking the expensive classes forever. While talking to Charlene about her interest in medicine and her progress toward certification, an underlying sense of doom would inevitably emerge. She'd reached the point in her training where she could start looking for work, but something kept her from taking a chance on her future. A bleached blonde with the hint of a Georgia accent, Charlene was the perkiest of the gourmet group and the most spontaneous of any amateur gourmet. Everyone wanted to join in when she'd start to sing "Zip-A-Dee-Doo-Dah," which she did for no apparent reason every time we met. Something about Charlene and Rex was half a bubble off plumb, though nobody could ever be sure why.

The Wine Problem

THOUGH I DISCOVERED many valuable lessons about cooking, I quickly realized these dinners weren't an inexpensive way to learn. In theory they should have been cheap—virtually free—as all the participants bought their own ingredients. All I had to do was provide the gathering space and watch them cook. Unfortunately, several things conspired to add to the expense. Thus far, I had been having trouble getting anyone else to host, and to use my little house, I had to have a stockpile of cooking supplies on hand. Any freelance writer will tell you there usually isn't a lot of spare cash available when you're starting up your business. At times I lived month to month, sometimes going to the bank for a thirty- or sixty-day swing loan to meet current expenses, rather than running up my credit cards.

Before each dinner, I would easily blow a hundred dollars at the grocery store so the basic supplies I lacked would be available should people need them. What I originally had in mind was free cooking lessons, but the way I was spending, I could just as well have flown to Europe and enrolled in a famous cooking school to save money. Moreover, the problem with wine hadn't been straightened out. When we ran out at the South of France dinner, I again ended up buying more. This, even after assigning two couples to bring wine, with the explicit imperative to bring enough for fourteen thirsty people. At this rate, costs had to be cut or my gastronomic education would end abruptly.

I huddled with Bjorn, Lucretia, and several other core participants in my kitchen during the South of France dinner. Serious discussions are always best held in the kitchen, no matter what the subject. We quickly agreed that wine was an indispensable ingredient to the gourmet. It enriched the experience and went a long way in helping people like each other as well as they did. What could we do to make sure there would be enough wine to see us through an elaborate dinner next time?

"I mean, we're dealing with feeding an army here. Everything gets eaten up, and every drop of wine is drunk. I don't mind sponsoring these things, but I can't pay for them all myself," I said.

"It's tragic," Bjorn agreed nervously. "Running out of wine. Catastrophe. The Red Cross should run out of blood on a battlefield first. We must take decisive action."

In the end, the problem boiled down to determining how much wine to buy and for what price and deciding who would make those critical decisions. Lord knows, wine can cost as much as you want to pay. Complicating this was a few participants had no clue how much they consumed. Try telling some people that each one of them drinks an average of one whole bottle of wine over the course of an evening, and they can't believe it. A man who came just once pushed his broad shoulders into the conversation, gruffly saying, "You ran out of wine. People didn't like that—you ought to know it's part of the meal. You should have had some in reserve."

"I didn't think everybody was going to drink so much," I protested. "In any case, this is a group effort."

"*I*," he said, as if defending himself in a trial, "didn't drink all that much."

"About how many glasses of wine do you think you went through? Just you alone?"

"Me? Maybe two?"

Of course the fact that his wife was going to drive him home and that he was staggering around the kitchen drinking straight black coffee, testified he'd outdrunk most of the participants.

It seems like an awful lot out of context, but the average tallied out to one bottle per person over the course of the long evening. We were, however, careful to carpool with designated drivers and never had a problem.

After another hour of animated discussion—it became clear that wine is a subject every gourmet possesses insistent opinions about—we decided it was clear that one person should be in charge of the wine. Each participant would be asked to contribute to a fund for the next dinner, and the wine would be purchased with that. It seemed like a good idea to all as the quality of the selection could be assured. You either paid or didn't drink. A Cellar Master would be selected to make a systematic selection of wines to complement the meal. The number of wine drinkers would be divided into the total cost, and the wine problem would be solved. This would give me an additional opportunity to gain experience with wine, which was unmistakably a vital component to a complete dining experience.

I would also be saved from bankruptcy.

"But wait a minute. Calling this person the Cellar Master? That doesn't make sense. We must call the person in charge of the wines the sommelier," Lucretia insisted.

"No, the sommelier is the person who serves the wine in a restaurant, not the one who buys it for them," Rex said.

Bjorn searched his pockets for a cigarette, knowing he'd have to smoke outdoors. "No, that's the wine steward, that guy in the tux with the tin cup dangling around his neck who drinks some of your wine before you do. Or is that the food taster? Kings have food tasters to make sure they're not getting poisoned." He found a cigarette and started searching the kitchen for a match.

I tried to settle things, saying, "I vote for a noncontroversial name. Let's just call the position Cellar Master for the time being. Now, how low do you think we should keep the costs? Fifteen dollars each for the wine?"

Bjorn exploded, spilling a box of safety matches onto the floor. "What! For fifteen dollars each we'll be drinking drool, Sorensen! Twenty—make it at least twenty dollars each. At least!"

"All right, a twenty dollar maximum per person for the wine. Anybody got a problem with that?" Everyone agreed, settling the wine issue at last.

Tasty Kangaroomerangs

THIS FAR INTO my makeshift gastronomic education, I had started to realize how much I could learn from different sources. Aside from stoking up the stove and learning to cook by watching friends, encountering exceptional restaurants contributed to reshaping how I thought about food. Heading into the snowy mountains of Australia and unexpectedly finding a restaurant of unusual caliber came as a complete surprise.

On a trip Down Under, my friend Chris Berne and I got acquainted with Sydney, then rented a car for a two-day drive to Melbourne. Chris is Jay's brother, who I worked with in a political campaign and occasionally travel with. We stopped over in Canberra, the Australian capital, taking time to see the parliament buildings and museums. On the way down, I over-drove the right-hand-drive economy car, boiling the water out of the radiator twice by early evening. Americans who haven't rented a car abroad may not realize that most of them have stick shifts to save on gas, and don't always have the sealed radiator systems we're used to.

There's a lofty sense upon entering federal territories in most countries, and the Aussies give their capital a feeling of happy authority, as though they don't actually need a capital, they just happen to have one. Ample parkways careen through town. Lakes and fountains break up the landscape and soften the tone.

After filling up the radiator at a service station and asking directions, we took out a guidebook and steered ourselves around the city, looking for a place to spend the night. The odd entry in the list of accommodations was University House on the campus of the Australian National University. Scant details on the place indicated the rooms were reasonably priced and open to visitors not associated with the school. So we kept our eyes open for it, assuming the setup would be a severe concrete dorm with washrooms down the hall.

I hadn't seen a car overheat since when my dad used to hang a canvas water bag on the radiator of his old, poorly maintained station wagons for long trips, but this econo car was on its way to a third boil-out as we snaked around the convoluted roadways on the university campus, totally lost. We were just about to give up and head for a conventional hotel in the commercial district when I caught sight of a minute sign that read *University House*, with an arrow pointing into some trees. A minute later we parked in front of the covered walkway—part of the entrance to a modest white building with a tile roof. It had the feeling of stylish, low-pressure Palm Springs resort hotels in the days of Tyrone Power and David Niven.

Inside, we were welcomed into an efficient, charming lobby. Architects have forgotten how to design charm into buildings these days, so this had to have been saved from another era. It turned out University House not only had rooms available, but they were singles with their own baths. We'd hit town during session break, so very few people were in residence, and we could have our pick.

"And is there a café or someplace to get something to eat? Something quick?" I asked at the desk.

The young clerk, a graduate student working off his tuition, raised his eyebrows and motioned to a doorway behind him. "Boffins is open to university staff and guests here at University House. You're welcome, but you'll want to go fairly soon as it'll close in two hours."

"Two hours?" I said tiredly, trying to make a joke. "We ought to be able to eat in that length of time, unless there's really slow service." The clerk raised his eyebrows again, this time, as I read it, because there was something I didn't yet understand about his restaurant.

Chris and I headed up the stairs—stairs not just to get you to a higher floor, but a grand staircase that swept you up another level in style. It turned out this building was purposely built with the wide, important-looking staircases you see in movies, rather than relying primarily on elevators, to give it more the air of an aristocratic English college. Furthermore, the layout included a great hall, courtyards, gardens, and a fishpond. Apparently in the original drawings, there were even thoughts of providing quarters for a butler of the Master of University House.

It started to become clear what we'd stumbled into when we made our way back downstairs, then along the hallway at the far side of the lobby, and through the door marked Boffins. It opened into warm, inviting, wood-paneled rooms, oozing a formal milieu soaked with clubby comfort. The sense of being someplace special hung in the air. Quality tables and round-backed chairs were arranged in formal fashion, napkins were folded into a swirl before each seat, many forks and spoons laid perfectly square to the lines of the room.

A young lady flew at us like a dancer crossing a stage, carrying two tall red-and-black menus. "Good evening, welcome to Boffins. Is this your first visit with us?"

"Yes, we just drove in from Sydney," I said, still half in the car. "Boiled the water out of the radiator."

"Sorry to hear that. I hope you enjoy your stay," she said crisply.

As I opened the menu, I couldn't believe what I saw. I expected to order a steak sandwich with a choice between cottage fries and a baked potato. Instead, the first page announced:

Wines
To accompany your meal at BOFFINS
we invite you to choose among the fifty wines in our stock

Fifty wines! It turned out they had a walk-through cellar of Australian wines, ran a bottle shop, and held wine symposiums and regular wine tastings. The waitress politely explained, "University House, in the tradition of Oxford and Cambridge colleges, which it reflects, has had a long concern with wine."

We selected a Peter Dennis Shiraz, McLaren Vale, and sipped as my stunned eyes staggered through the offerings. A sampling of the appetizers read:

Duck Liver and Cognac Pâté
served with warm toast

Avocado and Turkey Salad
with crisp eggplant and a sweet chili dressing

Smoked Ocean Trout
with a wasabi dressing

Char-Grilled Baby Octopus

served with coriander and tomato salsa
Quail Galantine
on assorted lettuces with red currant sauce

Canadian Cured Salmon
with toast wafers and cream cheese

"What have we found here?" my traveling companion queried, nearly folding himself into the menu. "Look at what they serve. I want to order all of it just to see what it looks like."

"No wonder the clerk warned us we had only two hours to eat. Let's get a couple appetizers, at least a couple. I can't believe this."

The menu for dinner read, in part:

Vegetarian Meal
bonbons filled with dried fruits and cream cheese on
warm salad of almonds, celery and corn with balsamic
vinegar

Festive Baked Turkey Filet
with sherry jus and fresh cherry chutney

Escalopes of Pork Filet
brushed with Dijon mustard and crushed pecan nuts
with port wine sauce and mango salsa

Crisp Rice Paper Parcel of Lamb Loin
with rum-soaked apricots and prunes on a Bundaberg
Rum and rosemary glaze

Medallions of Kangaroo
on macadamia nut croutons with a sweet chili and red
currant sauce

Tasmanian Scallops and Prawns
pan-fried with coriander, garlic and ginger, finished
with capsicum, cherry tomatoes, cream and topped
with pastry

Rabbit Filet Pieces
with wild mushrooms and cream, flamed in brandy

Plait of Ocean Perch
in a pool of saffron beurre blanc

I could have spent the rest of my gastronomic life sitting right there, in Canberra, at Boffins, ordering one thing after another. Eating until I exploded. And the prices were entirely reasonable—half what I would have expected to be charged in the States, assuming I could even find Tasmanian scallops or medallions of kangaroo or macadamia nut croutons. Those were some of the dishes we ordered, sliding into them with the baby octopus appetizer. I asked the waitress about Boffins. How could such an outpost of charming colonialism flourish at the edge of the Outback? She was polite and formal and informed, but seemed entirely unaware of what a find this place was. She said only that it was run by the university and they tried to do well by their guests.

I've eaten in upscale restaurants since, many offering pricey, first-cabin menus in suffocating environments. Too often the end of the meal brought an enormous bill and left nothing memorable about the dining experience. At Boffins, I had the opposite experience. The staff didn't begin to comprehend how great everything was. To find out more about this place, when I got home, I dashed off a letter addressed to The Manager of the University House Restaurant, old fashioned as that may be to digital natives, there are times when it's the best way to approach a stately organization more formally, especially when you don't know who might be in charge and at that point having forgotten the name of the place.

In response I received an affable note on letterhead—another form of communication unknown to my children—from the urbane Master of University House, Dr. RRC de Crespigny. I envisioned the multi-initialed house master seated at an old wooden writing desk halfway around the world, wearing his cap and gown as he tutored an American tourist who had inadvertently spent the night in his digs.

Dr. de Crespigny explained Boffins, saying, "Essentially, we are an institution which was established as a long-term residential college, but which must now function as a viable commercial operation. There have been problems of adjustment over the years, but I believe we have now a reasonably good balance of interests and activities."

It turns out Boffins came into existence on the basic premise that, because there are staircases throughout the building, no sensible form of room service would be possible, so a space had to be set aside for a decent restaurant to provide breakfast. Once the dedicated space was established, lunch and dinner were offered to help the facility break even. Because the greater part of the clientele work at the university, the restaurant also needed to offer something to make them stay on to eat.

Dr. de Crespigny further clarified that the name Boffins was selected after a Canberra-wide competition. "It's a slightly facetious term for scholars and the backroom boys of science. It is both distinctive and cheerful. When staff answer the phone, the word Boffins makes them sound friendly. The soups are made fresh every day, and there is always a vegetarian plate, as well as made-up plates. There's also a plain meat dish for those not necessarily wanting a major culinary experience every mealtime." He stated the Boffins philosophy: "To use good ingredients, imaginatively presented but not excessively decorated, and the items on each dish should enhance and complement one another."

I couldn't imagine a master chef anywhere producing such a clear-cut explanation of what a restaurant is trying to accomplish. For this to come out of a university is urbane and fulfilling. Why does it have to be such a rare approach to dining?

November

Blooming in the Gastronomic Desert

I HAVE BEEN reluctant to admit to living in Minnesota while experiencing my gastronomic reconnaissance because, to put it mildly, it is not revered as an epicenter of innovative cooking.

Minnesota is an upbeat, relatively enlightened place with a fairly balanced economy. It's also home to blistering winters where the mercury can be permanently fixed at thermometer bottom for weeks on end. Ears burn. Glasses fog. Car tires freeze to the street. Recently, a snowstorm that dumped more than four feet of snow over Halloween weekend was followed by a second snowstorm leaving another four feet a month later—a slight exaggeration perhaps, but it felt like four feet. The combined pileups stayed on the ground until the end of May, when the last traces finally vanished.

I moved to Minnesota a long time ago, and while the food scene has changed for the better, there had been a long tradition that no one wanted to offend guests or relatives by cooking anything different from what they expected. From the time of the early settlers in the North Star State, legend has it that the ubiquitous form of dining is the hot dish—called a casserole anywhere else.

A hot dish is made of leftovers and things from cans, mixed together with rice, noodles, potatoes, or some other soft white ingredient. Most of the food in Minnesota was, at the time, either entirely white or had some large white component. Seasonings, other than salt and pepper, were not permitted. Water was added into the hot dish so it didn't get too dry, then the whole thing was covered with cheese and slid into the oven. A can of mushroom soup could be substituted for water if the chef wanted to hint at a flavor while keeping the color white. When a hot dish bubbled a lot, you knew it was done. That was the type of hot dish expected at events from Easter brunch to Thanksgiving dinner to a Bar Mitzvah or just about anywhere else.

For dessert, the good people of Minnesota ate bars in those days. This dessert was ingrained in this frosty culture the way Sago palm pups are indigenous to the peoples of Papua New Guinea. Bars were prepared the same way as the hot dish, only they turn out flatter, gooier, and very sweet. Ingredients included bags of marshmallows and chocolate drops and nuts in any quantity. Minnesota cooks know that the taste of stale nuts is masked in most bar recipes.

Nobody really looked forward to eating bars or hot dishes, but as good Minnesotans, they were used to them. Neither of these staples had any particular flavor. Nothing distinguished one batch from another, but they invariably showed up at potlucks and parties and receptions because they didn't offend anybody. The more fashionable the event, the crustier the top of the hot dish and the stringier the goo when you pulled the bars apart.

Fortunately, Minnesota is home to individuals who've bloomed in this gastronomic desert. From what I can see, most of them come from other states. The majority of my gourmet group was drawn from people who had lived elsewhere for extended periods. I'm from California, Jay and his brother Chris from Ohio, others were native to Missouri, Chicago, and Georgia. Bjorn was raised on a farm at the edge of the prairie but traveled extensively. Bob Dute lived in Washington State while in the Coast Guard, and Mrs. Dute hailed from South Dakota. Gradually, she worked her way through progressively larger towns until arriving in the Twin Cities. She said she "snuck up on the big city."

At the dinners, the gourmet consensus was that native Minnesotans, including several who were present, are suspicious, fussy sorts, who prefer to be snowed in all the time. They are happiest when bombarded by harsh, stupefying weather that mercilessly thumps them and blows over trees. This was borne out by one native who said, "When it's really bad, I know things can only improve." Minnesota natives agreed totally, if not happily, with the outsiders' observations about them.

In theory it would have been easier and faster to learn to cook in a restaurant town. Were I to pick an ideal place it would be Chicago. Chicago is the best restaurant town in the country. It easily has a better, more affordable variety of restaurants than New York or San Francisco, which has a higher-profile culinary reputation.

I once heard Mayor Koch talking about the wonders of New York cuisine, saying, "Where else can you get a pastrami sandwich at four in the morning?"

I always wanted to ask him, "Where else would you need a pastrami sandwich at that hour, except New York?"

It is probably easier to learn cooking when there is more good cooking around, but it's not impossible. With the right people—even in Minnesota—it was possible to put together enough self-proclaimed gourmets to make the dinners work.

Germans Who Think They're French

THUS FAR, THE gourmet dinners held to European themes, beginning with Northern Italy, then moving to the South of France. During a midnight discussion in my kitchen at the tail end of the second dinner, Alsace-Lorraine was suggested for the third dinner, and several people hurried to endorse it.

"Alsace will be great. I knew we should do this," Bjorn said, always out front with his enthusiasm. I often thought of him as the group's shadow leader because he had answers to every question. And with every answer, he gave five additional opinions.

Jay didn't sound so sure. When I asked him what he thought, he said, "Alsace? I wouldn't know an Alsatian dish if I fell over it. Guess I can study up."

I wasn't exactly certain where Alsace might be either. I had the vague idea it followed the seam of France and Germany—one of the many disputed areas, perhaps? Did Hitler march into Alsace early in one of the wars? I tried to dredge up some memory of the place. The name sounded French—Lorraine certainly was—but there was some controversy within the group about the pronunciation. Was it "Al Sauce" or "Al Saise"?

It turns out both pronunciations are correct, according to the dictionaries I checked. Further investigation revealed Alsace is French: a region of northeastern France annexed in 1871 by Germany and recovered by France in 1919. It's the strip of the French border beginning where the Rhine flows north out of Switzerland to where the upper-right-hand corner of France tucks into Germany. The Vosges Mountains push the region toward Germany. The Rhine holds it back. Many delightful concoctions in Alsace are interpretations by France and Germany of each other's food and drink. It's said Alsatians even speak a German version of French.

Wine is the most common example of how these cultures come together. Alsatians make a German wine from a French point of view. Fruitiness appeals to German winemakers, whose product is for desserts and lounging around the back lawn in the early evening, while the Alsatians go for strength. Alsatian wines have more body and are designed to complement a fine dinner, particularly the cuisine of the region. Often they possess a spicy quality and a bouquet that comes from compressing the aroma of the lighter German grapes. Gewürztraminer wine sums up Alsace. These wines have a fruity scent that is clean, dry, and spicy, and goes well with rich Alsatian dishes. *Gewürz* means spice in German.

I asked to accompany the first Cellar Master on his pilgrimage to purchase the wine for the Alsatian dinner. Patrick picked me up in his ten-year-old Toyota. A deep gash of rust cut into the car's bottom panels, and the seats looked as though dogs had been fighting over them. The radio had to be smacked from underneath the dash to work.

"Get in," he growled, and we puttered off toward the store.

Patrick was an obvious choice to help form the gourmet dinner group, and he was with it from the start. He worked in the public relations department of a very large corporation producing videos. These were training videos, business-to-business communication pieces with a lot of talking heads. Vice presidents holding forth about this week's craze: productivity, quality, whatever was hot. This safe little job offered Patrick contact with corporate big shots without the downside of a heavy-duty management slot.

While I liked Patrick and felt I was building a strong camaraderie with him, he had his own personal Oort cloud clustered around his head. Theorized by Dutch astronomer Jan Hendrik Oort, an Oort cloud is that theoretical outer-space gathering of a hundred billion icy comets born of cold and gas and exotic turbulence outside the orbit of Pluto. Occasionally these comets alter their rotational velocities and streak through the solar system.

Patrick seemed surrounded by his own private Oort. He would regularly shoot off his own comets at people when they offended him. His insecurity came out as Oort anger. He would sputter remarks he'd later regret, get angry at the wrong person, and give a halfhearted apology a few days later, unexpectedly appearing thoughtful and concerned. Everyone has a friend they don't completely understand, or who is uncooperative, but who is still liked. That was Patrick.

Patrick guided his Toyota into the parking lot of the large specialty wine store. Inside, I pushed a shopping cart, Patrick curtly preceding me through the aisles. I felt the chill of his Oort. This was not going to be a good day.

"We'll start with three of these." He wrinkled his forehead, signaling an enormous decision taking place somewhere inside his head, the complexity of which he could not explain. Patrick continued picking through the bottles this way. Each time he stopped and perused a label, I asked what his criteria was for selecting the particular bottle, trying to get a handle on the method.

"You just have to know what to get," Patrick said, his Oort thickening. "You know, look, you know—you have to have done this for a while, then you know the wineries and the names of particular—you know— the particular wines."

"You know" wasn't enough of an explanation. I asked him to explain the choices to me a couple times and asked questions about various aspects of the information on the labels. Plenty of wine books spell out the details of label information, and I could study those, but I wanted insight—sophisticated firsthand interpretation—as facts don't always take when I'm just reading them over. But if there was an easy system to help me find my way around the wine racks, Patrick wasn't going to give me that information. leaving me to I strike out on my own.

Death Row

ONE OF THE perks of working my own schedule and having friends to visit in faraway places is the ability to indulge a curiosity. It seemed natural, with this flexibility, to spend some time unearthing clues to better understand wine.

I knew this much about the beverage end of organizing a gourmet dinner: There are four categories of adult drinks—beer, spirits, fortified wines, and wine. Wine offers the greatest range of subtleties and has earned the most elegant reputation. It is consumed by slow sipping with textures that change throughout the experience. A multitude of factors conspire to enhance wine and complicate understanding it. While any liquid containing sugar can be fermented with yeast, wine ferments itself. Yeast molds settle on grapes in the vineyards and work with the sugar in the grape to produce alcohol. The higher the sugar content, the more alcohol, which allows the winemaker to ascertain what the alcohol content of the wine will be before the grapes are even picked. Wine is classically organic and continues to change through its entire life.

Several wine store managers told me that a basic method of getting a handle on wine was recognizing the differences in the bottles. There are three basic shapes that categorize wine. Unfortunately, just because the shape is supposed to contain a certain type of wine doesn't mean it does. Many wineries choose a bottle they think looks cool. Shape is only a rough guide. There are no laws about who can put what into which shape bottle, so you can't be sure. The three shapes are:

Bordeaux: This is the pipe-shaped bottle that has the silhouette of a businessman in a straight-sided suit with high-padded shoulders. It was made famous by French winemakers in Bordeaux and is the most common type of bottle. It looks very serious and substantial and feels solid in your hands. All the major bottle types hold twenty-four ounces and pour about six servings. A typical wine glass is 10 ounces, which means you're expected to pour it a little less than half-full. Green glass is used for red wines and clear for whites. Almost every California cabernet, merlot, and zinfandel comes in these bottles.

Burgundy: This bottle is a little shorter than the Bordeaux, and the sides slope down to a slightly wider base. There's a good chance that Burgundy will be in these bottles, though it might be anything from a Rhone to pinot noir to a white.

Hock: These tall, narrow bottles traditionally carry Rieslings, Chenin Blancs, and Gewürztraminers. A bottle of this shape usually offers a sweet, light wine for dessert. Rhine wines come in brown, while Moselle and Alsatian wines come in green glass bottles.

This knowledge worked very well for me, at least as a starter. It makes it simple to hold forth about a wine without even looking at its label. Just examine the shape of the bottle and pass out a few phrases. You can get a lot of mileage out of holding a bottle up to the light and shaking your head, saying, "A typical hock, suggesting to me it'll be a little too sweet for the ratatouille."

I also asked an old friend for advice about wine.

Jeremy was my travel agent before he moved out of town. I had first met him as I stepped off an escalator in downtown Minneapolis and walked through a door marked International Travel. Inside the agency, I was directed to a thin, intense fellow leaning back in a beaten-up executive chair with stuffing coming out of several rips.

"I want to travel down to New Zealand."

"Oh, yeah?" He firmly tapped at his computer keyboard like Grumpy—the most contrary of the Seven Dwarfs.

"Can you get me there?"

Jeremy motioned for me to have a seat. "Oh, sure," he said. He was distracted by the flickering screen, criticized the airlines, and griped about South Pacific tour operators. I liked his assertive approach, which gave me some of the lowest-cost, best-organized traveling I've done. Jeremy wore unintentionally disheveled clothes—tweedy sport coats, high-water brown pants, and scuffed black shoes. He swore a lot too.

We occasionally went out to lunch, and I eventually met his longtime paramour, Marjorie, who sold resistors to electronics manufacturers. "And capacitors," Jeremy would insist. "She sells resistors and capacitors."

Marjorie, thin with ink-black hair, wore red when I met them for dinner—typically flaming red nylons, a heavy red embroidered shift with matching scarf, and black knee-high boots.

"How would you describe that shift?" I asked.

"It's pretty, warm, comfortable, and red."

It was a pleasure to go to dinner with them. They consistently tracked down good restaurants, driving miles out of their way to find them. Jeremy and Marjorie were also into wine, but in a different way from other do-it-yourself connoisseurs. They didn't need the very best bottles all the time. They knew few details about vintages, vineyard soils, the microenvironments, or appellations of the winemakers, but it didn't seem to matter.

When I visited, I asked Jeremy and Marjorie if they had a philosophy about buying wine. Did they have a system they used to select the wine they stored?

"We made wine a priority. Not by sitting down and deciding to do it. Just by enjoying a bottle maybe three times a week," Marjorie told me. "Jeremy and I will split a bottle with dinner. If we like it, we buy more, either find it on sale or get a case price. It really becomes a part of your routine. Something we do without any ceremony."

"Yeah, no ceremony, but it's a major event. Have you seen this?" Jeremy led me back into the spare bedroom in their apartment. They'd moved down to Evanston, just north of Chicago. Marjorie still sold resistors, and Jeremy got a gig repping group packages for a Swiss hotel. They rented a huge apartment, the whole third floor, nearly 2,000 square feet. It had two baths, a large kitchen, a spacious living room, and in the corner of the smaller third bedroom, amid cat toys, boxes of books, a doll collection in a glass-faced cabinet, and travel posters of

European capitals, stood something that looked like a portable closet. It was covered with vinyl wood-grain and required a key to open.

Jeremy pulled the handle and stood out of the way so I could admire the contents. The inside looked much sturdier than the exterior, with movable shelves capable of bearing the weight of 110 bottles of wine. Once closed, the door sealed tightly, and a small cooling unit kept the contents at an even temperature. "We have it set for 55 degrees. That's about right for reds. You want to store them between 50 degrees and 55 degrees all the time. If we didn't have this cave, the wine would cook in the summertime. It gets over 100 degrees in August, and that would ruin the wine. You've got to have a cave."

I like the term *cave* as a place to store wine. It suggests monks and catacombs cut into the rock under a monastery where bottles patiently mature over the years and can be plucked when ripened.

This cave only hinted at what Jeremy and Marjorie kept in storage. They also rented a commercial wine locker in a downtown warehouse with heavy security. Closed-circuit cameras watched the space at all times, and the individual lockers were secured with their own locks. They were able to store another six hundred bottles at this remote location.

Jeremy explained, "We're building our collection slowly in the warehouse. There's a lot of people using this kind of facility. Especially small restaurants and expense-conscious collectors like us."

I learned these weren't the only options for storage when another friend told me about his father's sudden enthusiasm for collecting wine. This is the same family that built a short fairway and putting green in their backyard after the father got interested golf.

This time the father decided to dig his own wine cave in the basement. He briefly studied the house's foundation and tore a hole in the cinder blocks. Using this access point as a doorway, he started to dig. Like many do-it-yourself projects, his was sidetracked by occassional crises. Over the course of several years, he occasionally dug at the cave and enlisted the help of his wife and seven children in the excavation. He'd get inspired and shovel several bucketsful of dirt and leave them at the bottom of the basement stairs. He told everyone in the family to bring up a bucket of dirt the next time they happened to go down to the basement.

For the next five years, there were always new buckets of dirt sitting at the bottom of the basement stairs, waiting for the next person who came by. No word on whether the cave ever stored a single bottle of wine—or how the man might enlist his large family to help him do something more complicated, like reroof the house.

I appreciated knowing all these storage techniques. However, I was still looking for some simple, straightforward advice for buying wine. Something I could remember without getting lost in details or interpretation. When I asked for the Jeremy-and-Marjorie selection system, they didn't immediately have one.

"A system," Jeremy said with an undertone of grumpiness. "No. Marjorie and I don't have a system." But after they thought it over, they found they could give me some guidelines.

On my next visit, Jeremy checked over the wine in the cave in the spare bedroom and locked its door. "I've been thinking about your question on selection criteria. I think it's all based on what you can afford. Anybody can throw money at wine—big deal. Throw a credit card at the clerk and don't think about it. It doesn't mean anything when you do that. Marjorie and I like to look for sales, look for bargains and take advantage of them. Then we get quantities we can consume over their lifetime. If you buy the right wines, which'll get better with time, you can buy them now when they're cheap, and let them age. You end up drinking a sixty-dollar wine in ten years that you only spent eight dollars on—that's the fun of it."

"But how do you actually go about deciding what to buy?" I asked. "When I'm standing in the middle of a wine store, it's a blur of labels and price tags. I look for cute labels with frogs, mountains, or hawks on them."

"You learn by drinking and trying it out. Ask the experts in wine stores for good deals. They're working with the stuff every day. They gotta know something. And read one of the wine publications like *The*

Wine Spectator—they'll tell you what to buy and when to drink it. Of course, they accept advertising so you don't know how much they're being influenced. Probably plenty. And you know another good thing about living in a state where there are stricter liquor laws than, say, California, where you can buy wine in gas stations? It makes the places that do sell wine specialize. Since wine is all they sell, they're more apt to know about what they've got. In Minnesota and Illinois, they have big specialty stores with well-informed staffs."

When I asked which wine store they thought was the best in Chicago, Jeremy and Marjorie interrupted one another blurting, "Sam's."

When I visit Chicago, I sleep on the couch at the apartment of my buddy Joey, a television director. During one trip, the producers he works with bought him an expensive gift bottle of wine, which wouldn't mature for ten years. We drove up to Evanston and had Jeremy and Marjorie store the precious bottle in their cave for him. Then we took a junket to Sam's.

Sam's resided in an unassuming building, a brick strip mall that gave no hint of what's inside. It could have been a waterbed showroom or a restaurant supply warehouse from the look of it. Joey and I climbed out of his impossibly tiny Miata, bracing ourselves against a sharp wind. I expected an overly neat shop with wooden racks and signs printed on white cards and a clerk in an ironed apron with an embossed name tag politely dusting bottles.

As we pushed open the door, we were transported into another dimension, a world saturated with Bohemian ethos. Between the floor and concrete ceiling beams rose canyons of wine. Looking in any direction—down, sideways, to the stars—I saw wine. Wine stacked in cardboard boxes and wooden crates. Wine creating a wall in front of me. Wine at my feet. Wine punctuated by filing cabinets, plumbing pipes, and a conveyor belt carrying boxes skyward at an angle. Newspaper clippings of vineyard stories, weird wine-related events, and comic strips were taped on boxes alongside hand-lettered signs defining the different categories of wine.

Patrons wearing everything from blue blazers to sweatpants and jogging shoes strolled intently though narrow aisles, carrying plastic baskets slung over their arms or pushing small shopping carts. No smiles. It's serious business at Sam's. Shoppers had the studied expressions of pilgrims searching for biblical truths. Pious customers shopped among casual staff, who dressed any way they wanted, usually in jeans and beat-up shirts. Neither Joey nor I had ever seen a wine selection of this depth. We could walk down a row and choose among seven or eight vintages from the same winery. There were sections for different countries and states and breakdowns by wine type to the point where I started to get blurry again. Where do you start with all this? How do you start your own cave and stock it with wine?

"What, sir?"

"I'm sorry, was I talking to myself?" I turned to face a substantial man wearing a *Ren & Stimpy* T-shirt, brilliant cartoon characters vaulting across the front. A large silver skull ring bulged from his hand, and a diamond stud highlighted an earlobe, flashing against his black skin. His biceps were mountainous. I would have thought he might have a Harley idling outside and wouldn't have guessed he worked there were it not for the price-sticker machine hanging in a holster from his belt. His voice belied his appearance, for it broadcast the well-spoken quality of a cultured aristocrat. His name was Charles, and he'd been a wine specialist for fourteen years—five of those at Sam's.

"You were wondering, sir, about selection?" Charles asked. "Could I answer a specific question, or was there something general you wanted to ask?"

"How—" I tried to organize my thoughts, "do I start putting together a wine selection of my own? What's the best way to start my own cave?"

"Your own cave." He allowed the corners of his mouth to turn up. "I'm not sure there is a right way. You have to trust yourself is the main thing. Don't go by what other people tell you. No one person can know everything or guess right. I misjudge how trends will run all the time. I thought zinfandels were going to be a fad that would blow over when they first came out, and look at them now." He gestured toward an expansive selection of zins on a rack behind me. "Don't be afraid to taste things, and keep your goals within reason. So far as organizing your collection, I have my best wines in a closet that I peek into occasionally but seldom touch. That's my cave, so to speak."

"Your cave?"

"Those wines will sit in there for a very long time. I just peek in, that's it. Then I have Death Row." His voice deepened reverently. "These are the wines I'm going to drink soon. When I put a wine on Death Row, its days are numbered. It's not going to last."

I liked the idea of those wines on Death Row, scheduled to be drunk soon, with other special bottles waiting in a cave for their time to come. I also liked getting advice from such a surprising character, one who looked like a biker and sounded like a philosopher. I pressed Charles about how to build up my inventory of wines. "What're some good rules?"

"First, you have to qualify on price. Then don't be afraid to taste things. You be the judge. Look around and have fun with it. Don't be dissecting all the time. I know people who are dour and dissecting, and they don't enjoy it. Eventually you'll begin to tell the differences between the wines that are aged in toasted oak and those with a dry finish and all the variations. Little things in making wine mean a lot, and you'll start to recognize this. You'll learn how to identify all the qualities a wine can have, give them names, you know—earthy undertones, notes of raspberry, fruity, young. You'll get the hang of it."

Charles' specifics about starting a wine cave from scratch concentrated on reds, emphasizing again that serious wine drinkers don't waste much time worrying about white wines. Once it's determined how much you have to spend, Charles suggested following these steps and staying within budget:

1. Buy medium-priced Bordeaux because they'll appreciate.

2. Go after better California cabernets. Look for upper-end wineries and vintages to cellar for up to ten years.

3. Get some whites, but don't go crazy. The Italians are inconsistent, but some California chardonnays would be good to have on hand.

4. Buy some Rieslings and Alsatians, but not so many you're going to worry about them.

Using his advice, I began to stock my cave.

Bottle in a Restaurant

ONE NUISANCE ABOUT drinking wine in restaurants is the whole routine built around uncorking the bottle and tasting it. I thought this needed demystification so I asked, wherever I could, about the right way to slide through this obligatory routine. I figured there is no reason to suffer when you're supposed to be enjoying yourself. There had to be a way to do this without feeling like I was trying on underwear in public.

The ritual of tasting wine began in a time when getting a good bottle was chancier. It isn't at all necessary to check for bad bottles since they just aren't that common anymore. However, one could crop up, and tasting is a tradition, so the game goes on.

I always feel like a real nincompoop sitting by while a waiter has me taste a cheap bottle of wine. After much duress, I streamlined the process when the waiter brings the bottle, I read the label quietly to make sure we didn't get any of our chateaus mixed up. This routine not only helped me learn more about wines and labels, but I've caught errors on a couple occasions where a busy restaurateur pulled a similarly spelled wine off the rack and was hurrying to open it when I pointed out the switch. Those are wonderful moments in an expensive restaurant. There's nothing more satisfying in gastronomy than catching an expert's error.

The uncorking itself can be arduous to watch if the waiter is experienced, but I play the game. Once the cork is pulled and handed over, you're supposed to sniff it to ferret out any moldy smells. You can roll it between your fingers and listen to it squeak to learn if it's damp and has been properly sealing the bottle all these long years—but frankly, why bother except for show? It does lend a certain air of noblesse, while on the practical side, I save the cork in case we don't finish the wine. Most restaurants let you shove the cork back in the bottle and take what's left home, whether or not permitted by local laws.

Jeremy and Marjorie always call a restaurant to see if they can bring their own wine. Whenever possible, they select from their cave, turn the bag of bottles over to the wine steward, and are charged a corking fee. Restaurants make a monster markup on wine, so many of them are reluctant or utterly unwilling to let you bring your own.

When the waiter or sommelier or cellar master pours a little into a glass, study it in the light, enjoying the color and checking for floating debris. Most of what you're looking for during this part of the examination is bits of cork, mold, or sediment. Unfiltered wines may have a few flecks of silt in them. A little sediment is not necessarily bad news. Filtering subtracts flavor from wine, so better wineries skip that step. Slide the glass around in a circle on the tabletop to stir up the fragrance, and stick your nose down into it, up to your nostrils. Taste a little, and if there is a problem, send it back. Don't let the waiter or owner of the place make you drink it. The whole point in letting you try a wine is to give you the option of refusing it.

After Patrick and I had first gone wine shopping, I watched management bully some customers across the dining room in a tony restaurant. The waiter called for help because the couple questioned a bottle of wine. The beaming owner shot over and smelled the glass, tasted a little, then tried to blow them off, laughing at the idea that the wine in his restaurant had anything wrong with it. The customers dug in and refused to drink it, and the owner eventually relented and had it replaced. He ought to have accepted their verdict and found them another bottle, making a show of tasting it. It's rare that wine goes bad with contemporary corking techniques and specialized machinery, but it can happen.

Radio-Free Reggie

IT SEEMED NATURAL to me that guests invited to a gathering, specifically for preparing and serving gourmet food and wine, would create an atmosphere in which stimulating intellectual interchange could occur. I had hoped that would go without saying. We would cook, eat, and talk, adding a cerebral dimension to the experience in the style of an informal salon. This salon idea appealed to me.

The first salons sprang up as social gatherings in Paris, evolving into forums for intellectual discussion and social change. Few contemporary settings exist where people can mingle and exchange ideas fluidly, though a gourmet dinner would be the perfect place. Why couldn't a salon spontaneously occur here? Shouldn't we try to surround an extraordinary meal with lively conversation and a vibrant atmosphere? I imagined the individuals attracted to my gourmet dinner arriving with their thinking valves wide open, brains racing, trying to luxuriate in the maximum analytical, highbrow, savant experience. Learning to cook was a quest for me, so I assumed all other attendees would feel the same way. There would be an unspoken elevation in the conversation. Petty talk on everyday matters would be set aside, and the lofty goals of gourmet-ship would subdue common topics and ignite the group with an epicurean spark.

Unfortunately, the Alsatian dinner bogged down for the worst possible reason—we invited too many lawyers.

My dating life had improved very little by the third dinner, though I invited as my guest an attorney right out of law school who had just landed a job with a big downtown firm. I had gone out with Lana the lawyer a couple times, though we were never all that comfortable with one another.

Reggie, also a lawyer, and his wife, a doctor, were core members who wanted to invite a couple with whom they socialized—two more lawyers. And Reggie invited a third couple who were mutual friends of all the other lawyers, assuring me, "They will be very excellent people to invite because they are such good friends of mine."

The dinner at my house again began with a little bit of discussion about Alsace-Lorraine, making for the beginnings of a salon atmosphere that included much deliberation over the food. But the streams of consciousness of Reggie, Lana, and the four other lawyers spiraled into an ever-smaller circle toward the most claustrophobic topic possible. They talked law. Nothing else.

At first I couldn't figure out why the tone of the evening gradually became muted and dragged. The food was good, but the conversation turned dull as it got later—the opposite of what had happened at previous dinners. The accelerating boisterousness we'd experienced during the first two sessions never even took off. I didn't realize what had happened until Bjorn came over to me. With a glass of Gewürztraminer in his hand, he pulled me aside between courses during one of the built-in rest breaks when the lawyers pulled themselves to the far side of the room.

"Do you feel it?" Bjorn asked. He gave me little nods. "Do you know why it is? I don't have to tell you, do I?"

"The atmosphere?"

"It's terrible."

"What happened?"

"It's terrible. It's terrible, and it's obvious."

"I'm not following you," I replied, aware of the ennui though still insecure enough in my stewardship to think I had caused the problem, whatever it was that had gone wrong.

"You know it's them." Bjorn motioned to the far side of the room where the lawyers had accumulated. For the first time, I recognized that they had culled themselves from the group—standing in a knot the way pioneers circled the covered wagons for defense against the Indians. Drinks clutched, elbows jammed into their hips, they stood erect, heads faced forward, postures reminiscent of Wall Streeters in *New Yorker* cartoons. Their backs formed a wall to anyone who was not a registered attorney-at-law.

"You know, they've been like that since they came in." Bjorn fidgeted, his shoulders jerked, and his fingers opened and closed around his glass. "Nice people you invited—don't even talk to the rest of us. No, they don't."

"At least they brought Alsatian food. That was all right—most of it anyway."

"Their stuff's barely passable—no kidding—and now they're off on their own, talking about what? Talking about law. Their lawyer jobs. The cases they're working on, judges—lawyers always do that. They don't have any friends outside their law firms, and all they can talk to anybody about is themselves."

In the middle of Bjorn's tirade, his wife, Lucretia, came over and cut in. "The lawyers you invited are having their own little powwow. Don't they like anybody who lives in the real world?"

The close lawyer friends Reggie liked so much had arrived forty-five minutes into the hors d'oeuvres. They breezed in, huffing and puffing, hardly said hello to anybody, and zoomed to the stove.

"Our babysitter was late," the husband said unconvincingly as he unpacked a grocery bag. They'd obviously stopped by the store on the way for the ingredients of their entrée and were feverishly playing gastronomic catch-up as everyone stood around watching. They cooked with weird intensity, as if they had spent all Saturday afternoon dictating legal briefs into a tape recorder, which rendered them unable to carry on a human conversation. The pair totally focused on the black steam rising from my smoldering frying pan as if no one else was in the room.

Initially, I thought their arrival meant another good opportunity for me to find out how someone who really knew how to cook would go about it. They were starting from scratch, and I could watch the whole thing. Unfortunately, all I learned was how fast two lawyers could sear grease to the bottoms of pans to cook an off-target Alsatian chicken hash and leave it for me to clean up.

Two hours later, the lawyers continued to isolate themselves, destroying the spirit of a stimulating salon. Worse, they criticized the wine selection—loudly—which enraged Patrick's Oort. He mumbled from a distant corner, "Lawyers. I've got lawyers in my family. I didn't come here for this."

The more the lawyers lectured each other about the wine selection and how it didn't measure up, the more wine they gulped. Reggie took particular offense when I started to pour his glass from the wrong bottle. Even Lana the lawyer, who apparently had a hidden agenda of chumming up to her law firm pals, forgot the rest of us. She started criticizing the wine, following the lead of her firm's higher-ups.

Lucretia stepped in close between Bjorn and me. "There is no remedy for thoughtless guests except never to invite them back. However, it is your duty to retaliate against uppity lawyers who've wormed their way into your house on the pretense of being gourmets."

"Right," Bjorn said. "Let's do something."

It seemed like a good idea. My desire to do something about the lawyers was compounded by Reggie, who, since the first dinner in September, was doing less and less to endear himself to me. He always endowed what he said to me with a condescending edge. Reggie was Mr. Perfect: ever ready to tell someone else what to do to improve themselves. He got so gossipy at his law firm they called him "Radio-Free Reggie." Want everybody to know something? Just tell Reggie, he'll broadcast it.

Lucretia and Bjorn acted in unison. As I watched, they slowly moved toward the insulated circle of lawyers who continued to talk about their cases and different judges and especially the wine: how awful it was, what an insult to them that it wasn't up to their standards. They knew they deserved something better.

Gradually, Bjorn and Lucretia strolled into position, their backs nearly touching the circle.

"I know this woman," Lucretia said expressively, "who raises hawks. She likes the hawks because they go after live animals, flying eighty-five miles an hour in power dives. Talons sharp as razors." Some of the lawyers glanced at her. "Sometimes we go out into the woods with one of her hawks and try to stir up some rabbits so the hawk can swoop down on them. It's good because they eat raw meat. Fresh meat—fresh, warm-blooded meat—it lubricates the bird." She went on in detail about what it looked like when a hawk sunk its claws into the back of a rabbit, the way the bird tears the flesh from the animal, spilling its blue entrails as it rises into the sky. "Do you know what a rabbit scream sounds like? *Eeeeoooch!*"

Her high-pitched wail dislodged the Alsatian chicken hash in the lawyers' stomachs. Their tight circle started to break up as Bjorn added, "And did you know that sometimes this friend of Lucretia stops to pick up roadkill for her hawk? That's if she can identify the animal that's been run down. Sometimes you can't tell a possum from a raccoon when a truck has flattened it. Tire marks obscure the details." He went on to explain the anatomical characteristics of wild animals rolled flat by tractor-trailers and their significance to a hungry hawk.

We agreed never to invite another lawyer to a gourmet dinner. Had it not been for the lawyers, we might have paid more attention to the parsley linguini, salmon in red wine and shallot sauce, and the Choucroute.

Out of the Tent

ONE ESPECIALLY GOOD recipe surfaced that evening. Jay came up with it after a great deal of investigation into what constituted an authentic Alsatian dish. It worried him a great deal that he had a gap in his knowledge of cooking, and he expressed great relief that he'd successfully created this dish.

I watched him go through the final stages of preparation. As he slid the pan into the oven, he explained what he'd discovered.

"It turns out the Alsatians have a fierce penchant for asparagus. They wait for it all winter. Some of them check their asparagus plots every day in spring to see if anything's coming up. Then, when the asparagus arrives, all Alsace-Lorraine goes wild for a six-week celebration. They cook it a thousand different ways." Jay sighed, imagining the huge asparagus festival spread out across the countryside. "It worries me, though, that they can get this wild about a vegetable like asparagus."

"How's that?" I asked.

"I just hate to think what happens when their cabbage comes in."

A Thoroughly Alsatian Quiche

Serves 6

Prepare the crust

- ✓ 6 ounces cream cheese, softened

- ✓ 1¼ cup butter

- ✓ 2 teaspoons heavy cream

- ✓ 1¼ cups flour

- ✓ ¼ teaspoon salt

Mix together cream cheese and butter until blended. Add the heavy cream and beat 1 to 2 minutes; gradually add flour and salt, blending with a pastry cutter.

When thoroughly combined, form dough into ball and wrap in waxed paper. Chill 1 hour. Roll dough out to fit into a 12-inch quiche pan. Line with foil and add a layer of dry rice or beans to weigh down foil.

Bake crust at 400° for 8 minutes. Remove the beans/rice and foil. Bake 5 minutes more or until set but not browned. Set aside.

Prepare the filling

- ✓ 1 pound asparagus, about 30 thin spears. The thinner the asparagus spear, the tastier.

- ✓ 1 cup whipping cream

- ✓ 1 cup milk

- ✓ 4 eggs

- ✓ 1 teaspoon ground nutmeg

- ✓ Pepper

- ✓ ⅓ cup chopped leek, white part only

- ✓ 2 cups grated gruyere cheese

- ✓ 1½ cups smoked bacon, cubed and cooked

- ✓ 1 pastry crust

Snap off and discard bottoms of asparagus spears. Cook spears in boiling water for 8 to 10 minutes, until tender yet crisp. Rinse in cold water. Cut off top 3" of asparagus and set aside. Add remaining parts of asparagus to food processor bowl. If sections are longer than 2", cut in half.

Add cream, milk, eggs, nutmeg, and pepper to processor and pulse to puree and blend ingredients. If you don't have a processor, use a knife, whisk, and bowl and start chopping.

Sprinkle cheese and bacon into pastry shell. Top with chopped leeks. Pour the egg/cream/asparagus mixture into the crust shell. Arrange asparagus tops in spoke pattern atop filling, creating a delightful visual effect. Bake at 400° for 35 to 40 minutes, until filling is set and top begins to brown. Let cool slightly before serving. Serves well at room temperature.

Eva Strikes Back

I LEANED OVER the fence, jacket zipped up to my chin, and told Eva about Jay's recipe as the first flurries of snow began to fall.

"Oh, asparagus—that's our favorite. We just love fresh asparagus. Don't have any right now, but I use half the herb garden when I cook it." Eva dug her toe into the ground around the base of what was left of the herbs in late fall, as if one lone asparagus might have hidden itself among the cold brown plants in her garden.

"Do you have one asparagus recipe in particular you like? Something simple that uses a lot of your herb garden?"

"Heavens yes, George. Asparagus is the greatest."

Eva's Herb Garden Asparagus Lasagna

Here's the recipe just as my neighbor Eva gave it to me.

- ✓ 3 pounds asparagus. Pick and save a week's cuttings from your garden.

- ✓ Herbs: Chervil, thyme, summer savory, parsley, and chives.

- ✓ Fresh herb bouquets for garnish

- ✓ 2 11-ounce cans cream of chicken soup, low-salt

Use low-salt cream of mushroom soup for the vegetarian version.

You can also use cream of asparagus, celery, or onion, and enhance with 2 or 3 tablespoons chopped European wild mushrooms, no soaking necessary.

- ✓ 1 cup milk

- ✓ ½ cup yogurt

- ✓ 1½ cups Parmesan cheese, grated

- ✓ 16 ounces mozzarella cheese, grated

- ✓ ½ teaspoon white pepper

- ✓ ½ teaspoon lemon peel, finely grated (Spice Islands is great)

- ✓ 1 teaspoon dried chervil (3 teaspoons fresh), crushed

- ✓ 1 teaspoon dried thyme (3 teaspoons fresh), crushed

- ✓ 1 teaspoon summer savory (3 teaspoons fresh), crushed

- ✓ 1 package no-boil lasagna

- ✓ 2 tablespoons parsley, chopped fine

- ✓ Small bunch of fresh chives

Steam asparagus until just tender, not limp. Cut into 1-inch pieces, reserve.

Make the sauce: Place soup in a large (2 quart) saucepan, add milk, yogurt, 1 cup of Parmesan cheese, cans of soup, lemon peel, and white pepper.

Over medium heat, stir slowly with a wire whisk to mix until smooth. Heat to a simmer, mixing well. Set aside. This makes about 4 cups of sauce.

Place about 3 sheets of lasagna noodles in a buttered 12 x 12 baking dish to cover the bottom. Layer 1½ cups sauce. Top with half of asparagus. Sprinkle asparagus with half the thyme, chervil, savory, and parsley. Rub spices through your fingers to release oils and flavor. Sprinkle with 6 ounces mozzarella cheese.

Repeat layers. Top with lasagna sheets, cover with sauce. Sprinkle with remaining mozzarella cheese, place chives over cheese in an interesting pattern, perhaps a checker-board, or just chop and sprinkle. Cover with the last of the Parmesan.

Bake at 350° about 45 minutes until bubbly and brown. Let set about 45 minutes. Cut into squares. It is wonderful to make ahead and reheat in the microwave. Garnish each piece with a flowered herb bouquet. Any fresh herb will work just fine.

It is possible to use fat-free cheese and yogurt but be careful that the brand you pick doesn't try to kick up the flavor by adding a lot more salt.

December

Filberts Roasting on an Open Fire

WHILE TIDYING UP after Jay's asparagus quiche, Lucretia approached me carrying her calendar. "It's going to be December soon—we have to plan." A surge moved through the crowd as word spread. The miniature tidal wave of response left no question about the motif for the fourth gourmet dinner. No dissension. No discussion. December's theme would deal with Christmas. "It'll have to be an all-out Victorian feast, nothing less," Lucretia said. "A traditional Christmas dinner."

Though none of us had actually attended anything like a traditional Christmas feast, we knew exactly what she meant. It would be the kind of dinner in those old movies set in hunting lodges with oak beams: a big, long, wooden table and food all down the middle of it, muscular hunting dogs begging for scraps, a giant chandelier burning with one hundred candles, waiters in knickers lugging silver trays mounded with food before a stone hearth. We wanted a fantasy.

"By acclamation?" I raised my arms, standing in the middle of my kitchen, asking for a vote as Charlene spontaneously burst into "God Rest Ye Merry Gentlemen." "Can we declare December the month for a Christmas dinner following the gastronomic teachings of Charles Dickens?"

"Hear, hear!"

"Pip-pip!"

"Jolly good!"

"God bless us, everyone!"

The spontaneous shouts confirmed the plan. The decision to create a gourmet Christmas dinner started visions of sugarplums dancing in everyone's heads. When it came to Christmas, we all came into it with expectations, none of which had anything to do with religious preference. Our Jewish cooks were more adamant about what should be on the menu and what atmosphere they wanted than the Episcopalians.

"We'll dress up for it," Lucretia added energetically, always looking for an opportunity to flaunt her wardrobe. Every time I thought I had seen the end of it, she'd trot out some new outfit. She ran her hands down her tiny hips. "We'll do costumes. I know just what I'll wear. I've got this gown with a neckline you won't believe." Her hands slashed a V from shoulders to navel. "And the most perfect pushup bra. It's Victorian—really. It'll pass. Dickens would have loved it. At last, a Christmas dinner the way it is supposed to be."

Bjorn made a stirring motion. "I'd like to prepare the wassail and a trifle. Make the whipped cream from scratch. You want whipped cream for Christmas, don't you, Sorensen?" Suggestions continued to flow until somebody mentioned a turkey, causing Jay to pipe in.

"We've got to have roast goose instead of turkey. This isn't Thanksgiving. That was last month, damn it. I'm not baking another turkey for a year, and that's that."

"I want to roast chestnuts," Mrs. Dute volunteered. "Does anybody know how to do that?"

"Chestnuts? How about an easier nut? Maybe filberts roasting on an open fire instead?" Bob Dute said.

"Really, does anybody know how to roast chestnuts?" Mrs. Dute asked, looking around at all the empty faces. "We have to have roast chestnuts. What are they, a lost art?"

"Chestnuts? I've never eaten one," Lucretia said as Bjorn shook his head.

Neither had I. Though we had always heard about them, no one had ever had anything to do with chestnuts. No one had even seen a chestnut tree or had a clue where to buy them, leaving me to wonder how they had become so ingrained in Christmas lore. Chestnuts were like Santa's flying reindeer—everybody talks about them, but nobody's actually seen the things.

Wanting to get it right, I looked into what made a traditional Christmas dinner. I found that Christmas is the prehistoric celebration of the winter solstice dressed up by Christianized Europeans who added trees, gift giving, elves, reindeer, Santa Claus, and stockings filled with lumps of coal. It began as a Stone Age festival timed to the shortest day of the year and was meant to symbolize the rebirth of the sun as the days began to lengthen. But even if the origin is celestial paganism, my ideal Christmas is a fantasy set in the world of Charles Dickens.

Anyone can prattle off his own version of a Charles Dickens Christmas menu, even though they've probably never even seen half the stuff and wouldn't recognize it—or eat it—if offered. Whatever the ingredients, the myth of a bountiful scene of a Dickens-style dinner is terribly attractive: the woody smells, a decorated tree, the cozy, snapping flames of the yuletide log. A beautifully set table where every soul is to be unconditionally welcome. People setting aside their differences even with a bordello of relatives they may not particularly want to see. A goofy uncle always manages to show up to dinner. Someone's third wife who brings the kids she had with her first two husbands finds her way to the gathering too.

Many writers have taken a shot at this holiday. One made a major success of it, and if he hadn't written anything else, it would be enough that Dickens created the ghosts of Christmas Past, Present, and Future, Ebenezer Scrooge, and Tiny Tim. With *A Christmas Carol* alone, Charles Dickens did more to help live theater than all the National Endowment grants ever awarded. Annual dramatizations of *A Christmas Carol* are so popular that perhaps half the theaters in the country couldn't keep their doors open the rest of the year if it weren't for the wild response they get from this one play.

My curiosity churned as I planned this month's dinner, propelling me to read more of Dickens' works. It surprised me how little I knew about the work of so famous an author. *Carol* isn't the only story Dickens wrote about this festival. He published many Christmas stories with sparkling vitality, most of them heavy on the social problems of his time. Some were very optimistic. In *Christmas at Dingley Dell*, Dickens paints an idyllic picture of Christmas reunions:

How many families whose members have been dispersed and scattered far and wide, in the restless struggles of life, are then reunited, and meet once again in that happy state of companionship and mutual good-will which is a source of such pure and unalloyed delight, and one so incompatible with the cares and sorrows of the world, that the religious belief of the most civilized nations, and the rude traditions of the roughest savages, alike number it among the first joys of a future condition of existence, provided for the blest and happy!

Among Dickens' other Christmas stories are: "A Christmas Tree," "What Christmas Is as We Grow Older," "The Holly Tree," "The Haunted House," "The Perils of Certain English Prisoners," "Wreck of the *Golden Mary*," "Mugby Junction," "Cricket on the Hearth," and "The Chimes."

Clues to creating our own authentic Dickens dinner were strewn about. In his story "The Seven Poor Travellers," Dickens described the procession of the Christmas feast:

> *Myself with the pitcher*
> *Ben with beer*
> *Inattentive boy with hot plates. Attentive boy with hot plates*
> *THE TURKEY.*
> *Female carrying sauces to be heated on the spot.*
> *THE BEEF.*
> *Man with tray on his head, containing vegetables and sundries*
> *Volunteer hostler from hotel, grinning,*
> *And rendering no assistance.*

I imagined recasting this procession with semi-cooperative members of our group and wondered how they might hold up.

Other stories are drearier, dwelling on class inequity. "Nobody's Story" is about the loud, showy Bigwig family. Another foreshadows the supernatural characters of *A Christmas Carol*. In "The Haunted House," there is a ghost in Master B's room and expeditions with a spirit who lectures those who don't behave about the possibility of their condemnation "to lying down with a skeleton every night and rising with it every morning." Additional punishment for the un-Christmased involves being sent to "a monstrous, cold, bare, school of big boys, where everything to eat and wear was thick and clumpy, without being enough, where everybody large and small was cruel."

Obviously, it would be best to be selective when borrowing Dickens' images to create a Christmas dinner. The more positive images were bound to work best. After getting into the spirit and gathering menu choices from the participants, I composed an announcement to bring the gourmet souls together.

Sorensen Gourmet Dinners Proudly Presents
A Charles Dickens Christmas

Location: Rex and Charlene's
Victorian Manor House
Date: Saturday 1 December - 6 p.m.
Please make reservations to use the oven

Our theme is Olde England—a Charles Dickens Christmas Dinner. Countryside England, the heart of London, the traditions, the hearty fare. You are invited to contribute your time, talent, cheer, and gourmet-prepared food to this feast.

As a regular or an alternate to the Gourmet Dinners, you are responsible for preparing a gourmet offering. To select which, fill out the form with your first and second choices. You will receive the complete menu.

Wine for this event will be selected by the Cellar Master. Patrick promises to take decorous care with this selection. And everyone contributes to a share of the wine. We have found this usually means between $10 and $12 per person—a little more or less depending on the selections. If you have any ideas about the wine selection, please call Patrick at work. Or call George, your organizer.

Please dress in the Charles Dickens spirit. And God bless us, everyone.

The Menu

Bob of the Bank and Mrs. Dute of the Shire of the Dakota: Chestnuts on an open fire with authentic English cheeses and other appropriate appetizers and mulled cider with brandy.

Patrick esq. and Guest: Vegetables of the King, potatoes of Ireland, his ancestral homestead, roots, grubs, and berries. Bubble and squeak. Patrick is also Cellar Master.

Mr. and Mrs. Bumble: Mr. Bleakstreet Soup, with true ingredients, guaranteed flavorful and bursting of invigoration.

George of Coconut Palms and Master Jay of the Mountains, and their Guests: A Christmas Goose, accented with oriental and Egyptian spices and the spirit of yuletide hi-ho.

Your hosts, Rex and Charlene: Pheasant Meat Pie, a delicacy without feathers you will enjoy.

Bjorn and Lucretia, who live together but have different last names—we assume then that they are only having an affair. Nevertheless, they will grace our table with both: Homemade breads and your dessert, a sumptuous steamed plum pudding with Cumberland sauce.

Some additional friends will bring other nutritious gourmet delights. Again, you will arrive promptly at 6 p.m. on Saturday 1 December this year of our Lord, at the Rex

House. And, of course, Jay Berne will arrive at 4:30 p.m.
to ensure we get to see him at all during the evening.

Finally, please dress in the Christmas spirit.

An Amish Rocket Scientist

AFTER BOB AND Mrs. Dute suggested it, who could resist? We
wanted chestnuts roasting on an open fire. No other nut would do. A
few members of the group had seen chestnuts at a distance, but we were
all sorely unfamiliar with the particulars of roasting them. They'd been
popular once, before something happened to the chestnut. Why had
they gone from being a Christmas staple to an obscure nut we never saw
anymore?

It occurred to me that I'd known a fellow a dozen years ago who told
me quite a lot about chestnuts. I had met Philip Rutter when he visited
town and stayed with my roommate. Rutter had moved from the Twin
Cities down to Canton, Minnesota, on the Iowa border, and established
Badgersett Research Farm with his wife. The two of them built a one-
room log cabin in the woods as a temporary shelter and soon had two
boys. Raising nuts and children and living in the woods without running
water gave Rutter an endless string of stories about his rustic life. Tidbits were pretty humorous, like when he put a lid over the crib so the
kids wouldn't crawl out and fall down the loft ladder. He told me that
one of the last things his son would say at night was, "Lid please,
Daddy." Without the lid on his crib, the kid couldn't sleep.

I remembered Rutter, a slender, brainy-looking man with close-
cropped hair and a long black beard. With his plain glasses and windy
explanations of biological theories, he took on the look of an Amish
rocket scientist—if such a person existed. His explanations of his theories took forever, with numbered points and diffuse thinking woven into
his tutorials, everything backed by facts, mountains of statistics accompanied each hypothesis. Sitting on our apartment's ragged couch long

ago, he'd said there were three to four billion chestnut trees spread across the American landscape until a blight obliterated them. These were once the dominant trees in our forests. He spoke at great length about chestnuts, working them into a smooth flow of biology, science, and social themes.

I wondered if Rutter still knew anything about nuts and, if after such a long time, I could still get in touch with him. I decided to try some conventional chestnut resources rather than try to track down and bother some people who probably weren't going to remember me. I hit upon an article in *National Geographic*, a piece titled "Chestnuts— Making a Comeback?" The lead photo was of the president and co-founder of the American Chestnut Foundation, Philip Rutter—the guy I had last seen sleeping on my floor. I imagined him living in the southern Minnesota forest, his beard grown to his knees, surrounded by nuts. He lived!

Rutter picked up on the first ring. It took a minute for him to dredge up the memory of who I was, but once reminded, he invited me down to Badgersett Research Farm, where they were at the height of Christmas tree–selling season. It turns out Christmas trees make a good sideline when breeding nut trees. If *breeding* is not exactly the precise term when discussing nut propagation, I was sure Rutter would straighten me out.

"You're still working with chestnuts?" I asked.

"Hazelnuts too. We're breeding hazelnuts as a cash crop and as windbreaks. We've been researching hazelnuts and have hybridized them to the point where we can propagate and sell them. Our new greenhouse will allow us to sell seedlings and seeds on a commercial scale," Rutter explained over the phone. "I'll get directions over to you on how to get here."

Hazelnuts and filberts are the same thing. The name *filbert* comes from the Frankish Abbott, St. Philibert, who died in 684 A.D. It was funny that our gourmet group had joked about roasting filberts over an open fire since they were Rutter's other nut.

I drove a couple hours toward the Iowa border, down a long stretch of highway with thin sheets of snow blowing across it. The scenery changed to hilly land in the southeast corner of Minnesota. I took a gravel road off the two-lane, turned onto a side road, and parked at the tree line. From there, a narrow dirt path snaked down into the woods.

Rutter didn't look a bit different from when I last saw him—same beard, studious glasses, big rubber-bottomed boots—and he still smelled like chimney smoke.

"Hello, George. Yeah, I remember you—come on in." The family still lived in the log cabin he'd described to me as a temporary building two children ago. The boys, now half-grown, sat on the floor playing video games. His wife was off selling Christmas trees out of their field.

"Temporary things turn into permanent things. Our cabin is a good example of that." Rutter motioned me over to sit at the table that served universally as a file for paperwork, a free-form mail-sorting station, an eating surface, a TV stand, a homework desk, and an office. Like everything in Rutter's world, it was part of a self-contained system. Rooftop solar cells charged a set of batteries holding power for the house, with a lawn mower-size gas generator for backup. Rutter wouldn't tie into commercial utility lines because the electricity came from nuclear power. There was no running water, leaving the family to slide water down the hill in plastic containers from a windmill-driven well. A wood stove provided heat.

The overall impression in the log cabin was of a family living in a tiny Noah's ark that ran aground ages ago. Rather than peering through portholes at a sandy beach, they looked out door-size windows into dense woods. A rustic ladder led to a sleeping loft. A hammock strung from the ceiling bulged with hazelnuts—hundreds of tagged net bags in the process of being sorted to track the trees with desirable characteristics. The hammock lent the decor an Abraham Lincoln–pioneer yachtsman aesthetic. An ancient upright piano sat buried under books in the corner. The overall footprint of the structure's ground floor was not fifteen paces long and ten paces across. There was no room for anything else. Even the chestnuts were stored, selected, identified, recorded in log books, and otherwise documented in a nearby shed.

Rutter dove into talking about chestnuts with solid logic and a profusion of scientific jargon and facts. "There was a time when a squirrel could travel from Maine to Georgia without touching the ground, jumping from the branch of one chestnut tree to another. They were that much a part of our forests. Then the blight hit, killing them. It didn't hit selectively. Rather, it obliterated virtually every tree. There were some efforts to beat the blight, but the US government let the chestnut program go bad. You let a research program run too long and it gets stale. It's the government's job to send in consultants and advisors to make sure that doesn't happen. Back in 1958, because there wasn't enough progress and the program was stale, funding ended. If they had kept funding it, we could probably have the blight beat by now."

He sat squarely in his straight-backed chair, explaining that the American Chestnut Foundation—of which he served as president for nine years—established a research farm in Virginia. It had initiated contacts with chestnut experts in China and Europe to make conquering the blight a worldwide effort. Rutter had been to China twice, traveling for hours into the mountains to gather wild nuts with the hope of locating specimens with blight-resistant qualities to be bred into American trees.

"What," I interjected in the politest way possible, "is the best way to select and roast chestnuts?"

In the same highly documented manner in which he'd explained everything else to me that afternoon, Rutter sat calmly in his hard wooden chair and didn't seem to take a breath as he continued his very logical discourse. "Remember, chestnuts have, traditionally and until relatively recently, been a popular foodstuff. This has been true since the days of the Roman Empire, when the price of chestnut flour was less than wheat flour. Most nuts in America are imported from Europe. This means they've traveled a great distance to be here and have suffered ill treatment from the uninformed during transit. So, with this in mind, there are several points to be aware of when broaching the chestnut issue as it relates to their consumption by castanophiles . . ."

1. Chestnuts should be stored like carrots, in a cool, damp environment. Too many grocers don't know this and let the nuts dry out, subjecting them to worms and mold. To check your chestnuts, to make sure they're fully hydrated, pinch the shell—if you can pinch a quarter of an inch, the nut is too dry. You want a firm nut with a tight shell that is hard as a rock.

2. After you buy your chestnuts, let them dry for two to three days so the starch in them starts to change to sugar. When you can pinch the shell about one-eighth inch, they're ready to eat.

3. Cut an X on the flat side of the chestnut so it won't explode when roasted. When one of these explodes, it isn't like popcorn popping—a baked potato–size *ka-blooey!* An exploding chestnut can do real damage.

4. Test the cooking time on the nuts. In a microwave, put a specific number of chestnuts in at full power for 4 or 5 minutes. Then allow them to cool down a little and peel the skin. Don't eat the brown skin, it's bitter. Cooking times vary with the size of the nut, moisture content, and power of the stove. When roasting on an open fire, place the chestnuts on the hearth, where they'll get exposure to steady heat without scorching.

Rutter also mentioned a dessert Europeans consider a favorite. Mont Blanc consists of pureed chestnuts mixed with sugar, water, cream, and other seasonings. He'd never had it himself, but talked about it as a distant goal—something he might indulge in once he helped beat the blight and there were plenty of chestnuts to go around.

All the Right Smells

REX AND CHARLENE volunteered to hold the Charles Dickens dinner at their house, bringing me great relief. This was my first break from
hosting, so I thought I would be free of the expense and responsibility
of arranging the dinner's details. This changed when Rex called, plead-
ing. "I've picked out a tree, and I'm not going to be able to handle it
myself." When I begged off, he insisted. "The dinners were your idea.
You want it to go well, don't you? You've got to help me get it indoors."

I arrived at Rex's place to find an enormous Christmas tree lying in
the driveway. It looked like the monster tree that dominates the front of
Rockefeller Plaza every year. Tall, wide, very full, covered with sharp
pinecones. Colossal in every dimension, it would fit inside very few
homes.

As I stood back, trying to take in the proportions of this pine, Rex
emerged from his house, smiling, looking neat, with creases in pants
that had just come back from the dry cleaner's.

"OK. You take the big end." Oh, thanks, I thought. He organized the
operation like a high school football coach motivating a one-man team,
telling me where to grab and when to push. Trees don't belong inside
houses—everybody knows that. Even so, at Rex's direction, I seized the
pine and ran it backwards, working the battering ram theory.

It was cold out. Icy. Tough to get traction. The front door didn't align
with the rooms inside, so the tree entered at a forty-five degree angle. I
suggested several times that it would be easier to cut it lengthwise and
glue the tree back together inside. "I don't think that would work," Rex
said, afraid I wasn't taking this seriously enough.

It took an hour to muscle the thing in, move it into place, and erect
and stabilize it with two-by-fours nailed into the trunk. It took another
hour to sweep up the pine needles and get the sap off my hands.

The small house, with the abnormally high living room ceiling and
the huge tree stuffed into it, looked like a timber exhibit in the Nature
Conservancy lobby. A stuffed Smokey Bear would have been the perfect
complement.

Throughout the rest of the week, Rex and Charlene went to great pains to decorate the colossal tree. They wrapped cardboard boxes in shiny paper to look like presents and tucked them underneath. Then they strung colored lights, hung bulbs, and suspended angels up in the branches. They also tied red and green ribbons on the windows, tacked mistletoe over the doorways, and taped holly onto the refrigerator.

As a finishing touch, Charlene warmed a potpourri of rose petals and herbs on the stove so the fragrance filled the house.

All-Night Goose

FRIDAY NIGHT I headed over to Jay's to prepare and roast two geese for the gourmet dinner the following day. We decided this should be a cooperative effort, given the expense, and because the master chef would guide me through the process. Jay lived on the top floor of a large house with three bedrooms. His space had a large living room, fireplace, and a decent-size kitchen—with a chipped linoleum floor and bad lighting. He preferred this living situation because it was affordable and included the companionship of two roommates. He welcomed me when I knocked, motioning me inside.

"In the back. They're thawing, George." Once in the kitchen he poured glasses of wine. "Do you think they're watching us?"

"The geese?" They looked like fleshy, entirely unappetizing lumps of fat sitting on the counter.

"Think they know what's in store for them?"

"I don't even know what's in store for me!"

We began by studying the geese from across the kitchen, reading the recipe, drinking wine, talking about camping and canoeing, discussing the gourmet dinners, and singing with the music we had playing. All in no particular order. We reinterpreted the recipe several times and chatted with one of his roommates, a young woman who was an engineer. She perched on a stool by the window, skeptically watching the daunting process of converting the uninspiring carcasses into the centerpieces of a Charles Dickens feast.

Our sottish anxiety progressed until we were impersonating Julia Child's voice with her lively errors, outbursts of humming, and fluid ad libs. Soon we marched back and forth across the kitchen, each of us carrying a goose, chanting like Julia.

"Respect the bird—respect the goose. Cook the bird—cook the goose. Hum, hum, hum." Talking to the geese, parading between the refrigerator and the stove, back and forth, again and again, humming, doing our impression of dear Julia.

After a long time, we tired, and Jay started stepping me though his procedures. He moved at his own modest velocity, a perfect speed for his cooking style and the right speed for his favorite pastime—camping alone, where he could get the most out of every crackle of the campfire, each whisper of the wind and bellow of a lonely moose. The more I followed his lead in preparing the geese, the more I slowed down and trusted my developing gourmet instincts.

The process took all night.

All-Night Goose

Serves 8 or more
We used two geese and doubled the ingredients.

Make the stuffing

- ✓ 2 apples, cored and chopped
- ✓ 1 onion, chopped
- ✓ 2 celery stalks, chopped.

Always be creative about the way things look when you're cutting them. Go for interesting shapes instead of always cubes.

- ✓ Pepper
- ✓ 1 10-pound goose
- ✓ Make the Sauce
- ✓ 1 tablespoon butter
- ✓ 1 tablespoon cooking oil
- ✓ 3 tablespoons minced shallots
- ✓ 2 tablespoons flour
- ✓ 1 cup chicken broth. You can make this from those little cubes, though canned or boxed is better
- ✓ 3 cups dry red wine. Never cook with a wine you wouldn't drink
- ✓ 1 bay leaf

Mix the stuffing ingredients in a bowl and set aside. Trim and discard any excess fat from the goose's neck and cavity opening.

Pat the goose dry and sprinkle inside and out with pepper. Trim tips of wings.

Fill the body with the stuffing and truss the bird. (This reminds me of an actor with opening-night jitters who, in the middle of the play, was supposed to say, "Let's truss him up with a tie!" He switched it around, saying, "Let's tie him up with a truss!")

Prick the bird all over with a fork to let fat escape while cooking. Place the goose in a roasting pan and stick it in the oven. Roast at 450° for 30 minutes.

Meanwhile, in saucepan, combine butter and oil. Heat until butter melts.

Add shallots and sauté until softened.

Stir in flour, cook and stir until mixture thickens.

Add chicken broth, wine, and bay leaf.

Cook to a boil and stir for 2 minutes, then set aside.

After roasting the goose for 30 minutes, remove from oven. Prick skin again all over and let the fat drain. With a baster and spoon, remove as much fat as possible from the pan.

Pour the wine sauce over the goose and return to oven. Reduce temperature to 350° and roast for 2 hours more, basting with the wine sauce every 15 minutes. However, some chefs have given up basting as they feel it lets too much hear out of the oven—so suit yourself.

If the goose begins to brown too quickly, cover with foil, lifting foil to baste. Cook until the legs of the goose move easily within the joints. (We cooked the geese for 30 minutes less, chilled them, then finished roasting the next day. We drained the grease and removed the stuffing and made the sauce ready to reheat.) Brush bird with a bit of oil before final roasting in 350° oven for 30 minutes.

Remove the goose from the oven and remove and discard the stuffing, let drain, then place on a serving platter. Strain the sauce from roasting pan into a bowl. Discard fat and return liquid to saucepan. Stir and heat.

Carve goose and serve, politely offering the sauce amongst the diners.

Bubble and Squeak

THE FOLLOWING EVENING, the dinner came together easily under a full moon that cut a disc in a crisp black sky.

Everyone dressed elegantly for the occasion. Lucretia outshined the lot with her low-cut gown of frills and ruffles and floor-sweeping hemline. She elaborately explained to everyone how she had contrived to smash together and raise her lentil-size breasts so they nearly popped out the front.

Carols played as the guests arrived. Bjorn brought a box full of vinyl record albums and a portable, retro record player. Bing Crosby, along with a dozen other performers, crooned "White Christmas." Every singer, it seems, has a Christmas album, and we heard them all.

Time flowed nicely. People floated in, and the conversation stayed light. Many spoke of Dickens as we carved the geese, which were reddish-brown and beautiful on the outside. We placed one in the center of the dining table. Red candles in crystal holders flanked it for show. Wine glasses sparkled in candlelight. Bob and Mrs. Dute stoked the flames in the fireplace, roasting the chestnuts according to nut-farm instructions.

One of the regulars prepared a potato dish that was called Bubble and Squeak because it made those sounds as it cooked on the stove. People crowded around the pot to listen and watch it cook. Bjorn and Lucretia created a plum pudding and a trifle—one bite of which packed enough calories to power a locomotive for a week. Charlene and Rex found enough out-of-season pheasant for a small pie and baked a letter P in the crust.

Several new cooks rotated in for the event and slid right into the spirit of the evening. Ricardo and his wife, Barbie, were back. She came in an elaborate, form-fitting, off-the-shoulder white dress.

Rex, who had shown an interest in her on previous evenings, couldn't keep his hands off. He nuzzled her neck, giving her a whiff of aftershave, radiating a big smile, cooing and fussing with her. "You look so pretty in that," he said over and over until people became too embarrassed to watch.

Otherwise, a dreamy quality took over, creating one of those evenings when kisses of happiness smack the air. A sense of joy, acceptance, and approval passed among the amateur gourmets. The happy mood rearranged the essence of each person so their best qualities blended perfectly as we feasted around the table. The brightest bubbles of each personality broke the surface.

Mrs. Dute sang after dinner, with Bob standing by appreciatively, even trying to sing a little himself. We all joined her in the carols, genuinely believing that we were doing what Charles Dickens would have done on a snowed-up evening in a Minnesota December. For the moment we forgot, "'Bah,' said Scrooge. 'Humbug!'" and remembered instead his sentiment: "I will honor Christmas in my heart and try to keep it all the year."

January

A Little Vague on the Details

THERE WERE TWO miracles that could not be explained, the first being the concept of a virgin birth, the second being what Rex did for a living.

A solution to the latter mystery presented itself when I got a call from Rex. At first I thought he wanted help wrestling the tree out of his house. Instead, the conversation turned into an over-rehearsed invitation for me to meet with him. Though we'd talked some about his entrepreneurial business activities in the past, details had always been a little vague. He'd gotten himself into something, but what? A growing business? An entrepreneurial enterprise? Since my freelance corporate communications writing career had taken off, I figured he wanted some input on a project he'd been developing.

"Would you like to get together to talk about some business ideas with some friends?" he asked.

"Some friends? What sort of business are you working on?" I wanted to explore this before agreeing to put any time in.

Rex gave a pat response. "We'll be working in the idea stage when we meet. You remember we were talking about some business ideas a few days ago. You're successful, and I want successful people to be involved."

"To discuss some business ideas?"

"Yes, I'd like you to come," Rex said.

I wasn't all that interested in getting involved in something so ambiguous. Many people like to picture themselves entrepreneurs and don't mind burning up other people's time because they don't realize that just having a good idea isn't enough. The hard part's making an idea work. But I agreed and skeptically showed up to talk about some business ideas. Why not give the guy a break, I thought, he's a fellow gastronome.

I wore jeans and a heavy jacket on that abominably cold night. The sun hadn't pried its way through the clouds in a week, and the mercury refused to crawl above zero. My car behaved like a hockey puck on the glare ice, driving to the address Rex gave me of an upstairs duplex in a marginal neighborhood. I climbed the stairs, surprised to find the place packed. Forty people crammed into the long, narrow living room, with a chalkboard propped on a portable tripod at one end. Some secondhand chairs were set in rows, along with commercial metal folding chairs that suggested some larger organization had been tapped to supply extra seating. All this made me suspicious as I had expected to meet informally with Rex and one or two business associates. As it was, I had my own pressing assignments to finish, and this was time I had taken off, I thought, to help a friend.

Everyone looked tired and nervous. Rex and most of the other men wore suits and ties. The wives wore Sunday school teacher dresses. These people sported so much polyester, they were liable to generate massive static shocks and electrocute each other should they accidentally brush together. Rex took my jacket as I entered, disappearing with it into the bedroom, leaving me with the legion of husband-and-wife combos torn from the pages of a defuncted Sears catalog. When he returned, he offered me some pink punch out of a glass bowl and gave me his together-guy, no-whiskers look.

I expressed my confusion. "What're all these people here about? I thought you wanted to talk over some stuff with some friends."

"Yes!"

"What's all this about?"

"You'll see. Let them explain." Rex motioned me toward the chalkboard. "Here, take a seat."

"I'd prefer to stand, thanks."

I noticed Charlene at the back by a built-in buffet. She wore a long party dress, frilly and pastel, not the dark colors people usually wore that time of year. Something was wrong with all this.

"Charlene," I said as I moved in beside her, hoping she'd take me into her confidence. "What's this all about?"

She fudged an answer, repeating something she'd obviously been told to say. "It's complicated. They'll tell you. It'll start soon." She pointed toward the front where the organizers were rounding everybody up, looking embarrassed as they did.

The seats filled, leaving a few of us standing around the periphery. The fellow who lived in this crummy apartment took the floor. He wore the plainest drab green suit possible, with a matching tie, and swayed anxiously as he introduced another, similarly dressed chum from a small town an hour north. I figured this evening's speaker must be a Big Gun to drive all the way down here in January weather and draw such a boffo crowd.

Big Gun jumped to his feet—actually leaving the ground for an instant—and started a high-voltage sales job geared to the path of least resistance. The very pat pitch started with a remembrance of his troubled "self-concept" and the way he'd borrowed money to pay his debts, only to "work my way back up from being in the hole to being worth nothing at all. I mean, I wasn't going anywhere, and I didn't even know how to get started going somewhere—ya know! Ya know!"

He went on like this, energetically pointing to the audience, putting everything he had into it. His maliciously blissful, expatiated discourse had the sucking power of a professional vacuum cleaner salesman who had found some dirt under a rich guy's Persian carpet.

I turned to Rex, whispering, "Is this a pyramid sales scam? Either Shaklee or Amway?" He froze, arms welded across his chest. He stretched his big smile and nodded, showing how pleased he was with himself for fooling me. "Where's my jacket? I'm outta here," I said, watching his smile melt away. A minute later I was hustled down the back stairs by several Amway functionaries who were afraid I would disrupt the deception.

Four days went by before Rex called. "Not to apologize," he explained. "I didn't call to apologize. I don't see anything wrong with inviting you to a meeting to tell you about what we do."

I tried to be understanding. "Whatever you do to me, don't waste my time. I asked you the purpose of the meeting, and you wouldn't tell me. Look, if you're not proud enough of the company you work for to admit who it is, I think there is something wrong with the shtick. Is that the only way you can entice people to join this thing? To trick them?"

"We aren't tricking them."

"What do you call it, then? You're selling tubes of rug cleaner and bottles of shampoo, aren't you? The guy who signed you up gets a cut, the guy who signed him up gets a cut—it's pyramid sales. There's nothing complicated about admitting that."

"Well, it's not exactly that. I'm building a business. My own business. I can look in the mirror in the morning and talk to my boss—me!"

"You're getting other people to sell soap for you." I didn't want to go through this drill. The first time I had been hit on by Amway zealots I was in high school, and here they were, still after me. Back then I thought it was a shifty organization that had trouble being open about what they were doing. I summed things up for Rex.

"Let me tell you the best definition of an Amway salesman I've ever heard." I cleared my throat for effect. "An Amway salesman is someone with a garage full of soap and no friends."

"Well, I don't think that's true."

"It is true, unfortunately. Because of things like this, Rex."

At least it cleared up the question of his livelihood.

Antipodal Juxtaposition

THE WEATHER DETERIORATED. Ice covered everything. A foot-thick, pasty frosting of slush covered the streets and sidewalks. Subzero snow dried out and crunched and squeaked under foot. Eyelashes froze. Glasses fogged. Ears burned. Snow crusted on windshield wipers, blinding drivers. Cars did not sound right because the cold contorted the metal so the parts did not fit the way they're supposed to. Entrepreneurs looking for their first felony raps stalked apartment buildings, waiting for people to run downstairs and start up their cars. When the drivers ran back upstairs, leaving the cars to warm up, the bad guys jumped in and drove away.

Minnesotans take all this with an odd, woeful countenance, arguing, at most, about whether St. Paul or Minneapolis has the best snow plowing. The process-oriented citizens hunker down and think about the fun of working their way through the changing winter landscape, while the goal-oriented citizens dream of what it will be like when those first warming rays of sun break through the clouds and the ice begins to drip off the roof. Just as it happens every month in Minnesota, someone said, "This weather isn't typical for this time of year."

Winter arrived in a big way that January, and it was very typical. Dark and cold. Very little sunlight. Awful wind. Cabin fever. Newspaper stories announced plans to tint the steam vapor rising from downtown heating plants pink to suggest warmth. Full-page ads ran for trips to St. Lucia, the Cayman Islands, and points south.

Amidst these obstacles, the planning for the next gourmet dinner went on.

The conversation determining what theme we'd try next usually began at the end of the last dinner, in this case heading out the door at Rex's house after the Dickens feast. Someone would realize the good time they'd had and begin the momentum. This time it was Mrs. Dute.

"We need to get away from European themes and cook something more . . . unpredictable," she said, avoiding the term *ethnic*. All food is ethnic, for heaven's sake.

"How about a broader topic? What about doing something like all the mountains or deserts?" Jay said, flushed with the success of the roast geese. He'd received waves of accolades over the course of the Dickens dinner and clearly wanted something more to sink his teeth into. "Let's do something bigger. A mountain range."

"An ecosystem? We might try a theme that'll give us more room to move around in," I said, but couldn't think of what that might be. You can't be specific and general at the same time.

"The whole earth?" Jay said.

"How about space food?" Charlene's lugubrious delivery tended to make whatever she said sound like a joke. Even so, several of the tribe nodded, evidently thinking of ways to simulate weightless conditions.

As the discussion continued, somebody suggested all the canyons in the world. Someone else suggested only food that flies. Bjorn thought we should just eat trees or narrow that down to plants that grow in the shade. Clearly we needed a theme of some kind to give definition, for without it, the cooks would play it safe, probably resort to preparing dishes they had cooked before. I was afraid the gourmet dinner would turn into a potluck if we didn't have focus. I thought the temptation to agree to a theme that was overly broad or silly could be just as big a problem.

This fear rocked me on my heels when fish was mentioned. Fish scared me. I felt even more afraid when the suggestion of fish broadened to include all seafood. Jay took a deep breath and shoved his fists into his pockets.

"Oh, hell, let's just make it a whole ocean. How about the Pacific? Or are we closer to the Atlantic here?"

Charlene liked the idea. "We're right in the middle between them. Let's make it both oceans. The oceans!"

Bjorn cut in, his hands at his hair. "Now wait a minute. There are technically oceans and seas. At least seven seas. We must be specific."

"But the seas are fresh water," Jay said.

"No, they're not. Now listen, all right?" Bjorn talked so fast he stuttered. "There's the Atlantic and Pacific, Indian, Arctic, and Antarctic oceans. And—" By now someone had broken out an atlas, and Bjorn started picking names. "—the seas are Yellow, Red, Black, Tasman, China—"

"Oh, stop," Lucretia insisted. "He gets this way."

"Philippine, Coral, Mediterranean—"

"Since when have you ever heard anybody call the Mediterranean a sea? It's just the Mediterranean," Lucretia insisted.

"The Caribbean Sea," Bjorn said stoutly. "Arabian, Timor, Arafura, North, Norwegian, Labrador, Beaufort, many more than seven."

I tried to reconcile the positions, "You want to do the oceans? If we just did the oceans, could that be a theme?"

"Would it include the coasts?" Lucretia asked.

"What about just doing the bottom of the oceans?" I said.

Jay, ever the naturalist, placed his hands over his eyes. "You don't want what's on the bottom of the oceans. Trust me. Don't eat that stuff. You've heard about bottom-feeders, haven't you?"

I wondered aloud how to refine the fish theme. "We could open this up. I mean, call it The Oceans. We'll have to trust that people won't screw around with it and bring chicken and call it 'chicken of the sea' or something like that."

Charlene stumbled ahead. "I can think of lotsa, lotsa, lotsa things to do with this oceans theme. Plenty. This is a good idea. And only saltwater, right?"

I started to set parameters. "Can we limit it to saltwater?" All agreed, leaving us with plenty of room for interpretation, since the oceans cover 71 percent of the earth's surface—nearly three-quarters of the total area. That is 61 percent of the surface in the Northern Hemisphere and 81 percent in the Southern Hemisphere.

The oceans, for what it's worth, are also in antipodal juxtaposition with the earth's land masses.

Under the Sea

BEFORE I REACHED college, my closest acquaintance with fish came from canned tuna. Tuna sandwiches were ubiquitous in households when I was growing up. Occasionally I would also heat frozen fish sticks in the toaster oven after school when we could get past the babysitters who spent their afternoons picking through the refrigerator. This fostered little understanding of the oceans. Fish sticks are about as far away from an actual fish as you can get. The brand we had were precooked with golden breading and formed into the shape of little wooden gangplanks, suggesting that fish were rectangular and lacked specific names like cod or halibut.

I've since learned the reasons my family never ate fish. One was my parents didn't have a clue how to cook it. Another was my father had spent some time in a tuna cannery, drawing pictures for a wall mural he would paint as a college art project. San Diego had a large tuna fleet at the time, and Dad made several trips to one of the processing plants to sketch albacore being gruesomely gutted, beheaded, scaled, deboned, and canned. Because he'd had to ride the streetcar home day after day smelling like the factory, our family could never eat fish. So he said.

Marinated Man-Eaters

THE OCEANS MOVED the dinners back to my house. I stocked the kitchen, made sure the Cellar Master got the wine, set the table, and turned up the heat.

Patrick arrived at The Oceans gourmet dinner dragging along a woman he called—behind her back—"the Fishmonger." She was a captive of his most recent siege on the girlfriend front. She walked in stiff-shouldered and dressed in a black skirt. Her raven hair was parted down the middle, falling to her shoulders. She spoke politely, obviously acting cautious with our group.

"The Oceans? How'd you come up with that?" she asked. Not the question you expect from someone who sells fish for a living.

"We take suggestions and reach a consensus," I explained.

"Oh, interesting," she replied, looking around the room and sniffing the fishy air.

Standing together, Patrick and the Fishmonger didn't seem like much of a couple. I had the feeling she'd come to The Oceans dinner more out of curiosity about we would-be gourmets than about him. Patrick had met the Fishmonger several months earlier at the farmers market, which was held on weekends in the area full of brick buildings in the lower town section of St. Paul. Growers drove in from the countryside to sell tomatoes, pumpkins, apples, corn, and whatever else is in season.

The Fishmonger operated a seafood distribution company and had a truck with fish from her booming retail seafood store. Patrick struck up a conversation with her while leaning over a tailgate loaded with shrimp and clams. Since they had met, he'd been building up to this invitation for what must have seemed the perfect dinner. After all, they could share their common interest in fish. Surely scores of couples enjoy long lives together with far less in common.

She supplied a large piece of shark to The Oceans. Patrick marinated it in lemon juice and cooked it on my outdoor grill, sloshing out into the snow and turning it over with his hands when she wasn't watching. All the time he cooked, he complained that I didn't have the seasonings he needed. Bring your own damn spices, Oort Man, I thought.

Besides Patrick offering a good example of how to mismanage a date, this turned out to be a good lesson on cooking because I discovered one can gather a great deal of gastronomic insight from what doesn't come out right. The shark proved to be a lesson on how not to cook fish, since we never had a dish so universally hated, detested, gossiped about, and refused. It pulled bad reviews for the marinade and for being under-cooked and for Patrick's attitude. Most people left the marinated man-eater on their plate after trying the tiniest bite. Word about bad fish travels fast.

It took a fair amount of experimentation on my own to realize that shark can be grilled deliciously, though I wouldn't have known given this introduction. Everything else served that evening went, well, swim-mingly. We sampled taramosalata, an appetizer of Greek origin, blended together over a pound of whole cod roe, cream cheese, garlic lemon juice, olive oil, heavy cream, and spices. We served baked redfish en papillote and Mediterranean eggplant with shrimp and dill sauce. I adapted a recipe for mussels steamed in wine sauce, trying to duplicate those I'd had sitting at the bar at Legal Seafood in Boston—it came close. Bjorn discovered a recipe called gravlax that his uncle had used to pre-pare raw salmon, curing it in sugars and spices. Learning all these reci-pes helped me conquer my fear of fish.

Jay even won a recipe contest sponsored by one of the local newspa-pers for his wild rice clam chowder. It is the best I've ever had.

Jay's Wild Rice Clam Chowder

Serving size: 8 or more

- ✓ 6 medium potatoes, peeled and cut into ½-inch cubes. The smaller the potato, the harder it is to peel. You can also use mashed potatoes in clam chowder and might want to try that sometime.

- ✓ 2 32-ounce boxes of salt-free chicken broth. One box is used for the chowder and the other for cooking the rice, and adding more liquid to the chowder if you need it.

- ✓ 2 6½-ounce cans minced clams—drain and retain liquid.

- ✓ Juice of ½ a lemon

- ✓ 3 bay leaves

6-quart stockpot, combine clam liquid, one box of chicken broth, potatoes, lemon juice, and bay leaves. Bring to a boil. Reduce heat and simmer 20 minutes.

Meanwhile, cook:

1 cup wild rice in 3 cups chicken broth from the second box for 30 minutes.

Drain the rice, if all the liquid was not absorbed, and set aside.

In a skillet, sauté:

- ✓ ¼ pound diced bacon

Bacon is best cooked leisurely over a low heat. Drain bacon, retaining half of drippings in the pan to cook in.

Add to the bacon drippings:

- ✓ 1½ medium onions, finely chopped
- ✓ ½ pound mushrooms, thickly sliced
- ✓ 3 tablespoons butter

Sauté until the onions are clear and the room is filled with the piquant aroma. Add 6 tablespoons fine flour to the onion mixture. Cook and stir to thicken.

Add to potatoes and broth, the bacon, cooked wild rice, clams, and onion-mushroom mixture. Stir in 1½ cups whipping cream and ¼ cup dry sherry. Heat through while stirring.

Toss a few oysterette crackers on top and serve.

Over to France

EIGHTEEN YEARS HAD passed since I'd last visited France, and I was only going now because my buddy Joey in Chicago racked up enough frequent-flyer credits to give me a free first-class ticket.

We flew into Nice and, after spending three days exploring the Cote d'Azur, took the super-speedy TGV train to Paris. After such a long absence, I sensed a huge difference the instant I stepped out of the station. I was no longer the long-haired kid who'd had his picture taken on the top of the Arc de Triomphe with a tired sneer, unable to afford the most modest café lunch on an undistinguished side street. I had grown into a middle-aged, midcareer man with credit cards that could bear the cost of a decent hotel—even a meal in a good restaurant. True, I was more experienced and older, but I sensed Paris and I had both changed. I still couldn't find the 1920s Paris that Hemingway described. The moveable feast had indeed vanished a long time ago, but in its place I discovered a different kind of city.

These days Paris is a permanent frat party for adults.

Every fifteen steps another restaurant sprouts, and chances are it's quite good. A bottle of wine is cheaper than a bottle of Coke. Peculiarities like little vacuum cars sucking up litter and dog debris while perfuming the sidewalks with scented water seemed cute. So did the public art tucked into cubbyholes and splattered across squares, and the city's slavish devotion to preserving an architectural heritage. I could stand for hours studying the flying buttresses, the gothic ribs of Notre Dame. Musée d'Orsay—a railway station beautiful in itself, converted into a cavernous museum—felt truly romantic. All of it seemed fun. This was an experience entirely different from that of Hemingway's or my youth. Most of the Parisians were quite civil, and though I hadn't taken a single French lesson in twenty years, they were able to understand me just fine.

Bolstered by these good vibes, I was prepared to go to an expensive restaurant and spend a lot of money. I felt pregnant with my newly discovered knowledge about cooking and eating and wanted to see if I would appreciate Paris more because of it. I wanted to be smashed into a little table with a bunch of people, listening to them discuss philosophy and the rigors of life. It would be OK if I couldn't understand half of what they said. I wanted to wear a hot tie and my Brooks Brothers blazer and feel underdressed looking toward one end of the room and too conservative looking toward the other.

One evening Joey and I headed out on a quest for my phenomenal restaurant. We began with a descent into the Metro, a model subway for the rest of the world. The quiet *whoosh* of rubber tires whisked the train into a station. The cars were clean and quiet. Many of the seats had curved backs so they fit people comfortably, instead of being sawmill-straight like the seats in General Motors cars and Boeing airliners.

We stepped into the second-class car, and the train took off. With so many restaurants to choose from, where would we begin? Why not try the restaurant in La Tour Eiffel? It's famous, easy to find. I had heard of one local who ate lunch there every day; he said he had to because it was the only place in the city from which he couldn't see the damned Eiffel Tower. But no, too touristy. I wanted boho and studied the Metro map, homing in on the Latin Quarter. This area had the surly, antisocial reputation I yearned for. The food there had to be good.

As we emerged from the Metro in the heart of the quarter, the wet streets reflected a blaze of red taillights, yellow streetlamps, pulsating signs from businesses, and roaring motor scooter backfire. People were everywhere—on the sidewalks, strolling the middle of the cobblestones, seated proudly in restaurant windows.

For the first time, I felt my new experience with cooking more-complicated meals made me comfortable evaluating a menu and exploring adventuresome dishes. For the first time, I felt up to the task of bugging out the offerings in a world-class restaurant. I would be able to—in theory—ask intelligent questions, order correctly, eat with enjoyment, and pay without feeling too ripped off. All the restaurants we passed posted menus, but as we crept from window to window, it was easier to tell from the expressions on the faces of the patrons how things were going inside than to attempt a translation of the French menus. Smart restaurateurs put the liveliest, most famous, most beautiful, and most obviously happy people by the front windows. If these front-window people didn't look content with the progress of their meal, things could only be worse deeper inside. This technique is used worldwide. In Los Angeles, they don't just put beautiful people in the window. To give customers more clues about their restaurant, they park the most expensive cars by the front door.

We cruised the Latin Quarter, got lost a couple times, and spent the better part of an hour studying restaurant windows. It really was difficult to make a selection among the attractive alternatives, and we decided by accident to walk into Le Procope. As in marriage, it is often better to choose by intuition than to make a conscious intelligent decision, as failures are far more spectacular when you go into them blindly.

I led the way in, gazing into the first of a series of rooms in what turned out to be a rather large restaurant. It hadn't looked that way from the outside. An elegant man in a black tux played cocktail piano on a worn upright situated in a foyer reminiscent of an old mansion. Behind him, a flight of stairs led to the powder rooms, while on either side were busy halls of small tables loaded with satisfied-looking diners.

"Do you take credit cards?" I asked. I felt like a dope for making that my first question, but not being able to put it into French and not seeing a Visa sticker on the door, I didn't want raspberries with créme anglaise to arrive and not have the cash to cover it.

"Yes! Credit cards!" a handsome man beamed, welcoming us into the room on the left. "Please, follow me." I immediately felt something I had never expected in a Paris restaurant—I experienced feeling welcome with an undercurrent of genuine anticipation. It was not just the food I expected Le Procope's chefs to prepare in some unusual way, serve elegantly, and let me savor. I truly believed this would be a total eat-in, one of those rare evenings I would have had if Humphrey Bogart had invited me into Rick's Café Américain, swept me over to an empty table near the piano, and said, "Enjoy yourself, kid. I think you'll like da place."

We were seated at the wall toward the middle of the brightly lit room. The tables sat close together. My immediate impression was that everyone was watching everyone else. All eyes continually wandered around, looking, without hesitation or the slightest embarrassment, into the faces of others, gauging the reactions to what they were eating, studying their tables, their clothes, the plates, how they liked dinner.

I studied the menu. Its enormous size made it fun to open in the tight space. Its tall, elegant blue cover bore a Republique Françoise 200-year anniversary logo: crossed ax blades and a pike with the traditional flopped-over red hat of the revolution. In a circle it said, "Restaurant le Procope, Fondé en 1686." I went on to discover that Procope billed itself the oldest café in the world.

Substantiating that claim, the menu explained that Francesco Procopio dei Coltelli of Palermo came to Paris and opened what became a meeting place for "the intellectual set, for people of sensibility—the first literary coffeehouse." Coffee being a new beverage in town at the tail end of the seventeenth century, as well as a social lubricant for liberal philosophers, the place became a hangout. Early diners at Le Procope included the Encyclopedists, Diderot, d'Alembert, and Benjamin Franklin. Procope also claimed linkage with other revolutionary thinkers: Robespierre, Danton, and Marat. The young lieutenant Napoleon Bonaparte allegedly left his hat there as a pledge—a pledge of what was not explained. The liveliness of the place told me that when they said, "Procope of today is still faithful to the memory of its distinguished past and its table of Voltaire—still on the premises—and is at once a symbol of a festimony of permanence, ready to welcome new distinctions," they meant it. What they meant by *festimony* I don't know, but it sounded important at the time.

Next, I wondered how and what I would order. The menu's large type bannered headlines in a bold serif font with the list of offerings beneath in flamboyant cursive script. At the top center, the headline *L'Ecailler* had a quotation in French from Flaubert next to it. I figured Flaubert's immortal line to mean, "Come and eat here once the hostilities are over."

House specialties were printed in red, the more common offerings in brown. *Les Poissons*; Fish. *Les Fromages*; Cheese. *Les Entrees*; same in English. *Les Fruits de Mer*; Fruit of the Sea. Oui, seafood—that was the way to go.

All around the room people had all sorts of fish, clams, shells, claws, so many sea creatures I thought Neptune had come to dine. I wanted something that had some zip. Something that I would be proud to be seen eating. Something to show my fellow Parisians that even if I had been raised to think good food meant greasy Swedish meatballs, I had learned—damn it, I had learned!

The waiter came over. "*Monsieur?*"

"*Les Fruits de Mer, garçon, s'il vous plait,*" I said.

The waiter nodded. "*Oui, monsieur, somethingIcoudn'tunderstand. Très bien. SomethingIcoudn'tunderstand. Bon.*"

"Oui," I said confidently and pointed to *Le Plateau Procope*. The price listed under this dish: pour 2 personness seemed like a lot. It was just about the most expensive thing on the menu, but I figured when you don't know what you're going to get, you might as well order by category and price. Unless this was a giant squid, I should be OK—my mind blanked. For an instant, I pictured a platter bearing several translucent tentacles sautéed in butter with hubcap-size suction cups oozing cream sauce.

We were into the wine list right away, picking by price and category again, and I forced the squid image out of my mind. This wine list was very straightforward, taking up half the back of the menu under the heading "*La Cave de Zoppi.*" In a box it listed wines from the Vallée du Rhône, *Procope savourait ces vins, nous les avons spécialement sélectionnés pour vous.* Below that, *Les Blancs, Les Roses, Les Rouges, Les Champagnes,* with these categories divided by region.

"*Vin Blanc, Muscadet sur Lie,*" I said. This wine was printed in red type, indicating it was a specialty from Val de Loire. I had learned something about buying wine in stores like Sam's in Chicago—as for ordering in restaurants, I wasn't as good. When I don't know any better, I select from a wine list the same way I choose a roofer: I take three bids and pick the one that is priced in the middle. Buy too cheap, and I get something I regret. Pay top price, and I'm never quite satisfied because it cost so much.

The first indication of what our *Le Plateau Procope* would grow into arrived with the waiter. He carefully positioned a circular metal frame on the table, towering ten inches over the tabletop, high above the salt and pepper shakers. He soon emerged from the kitchen carrying the largest round aluminum platter I have ever seen. It hovered like a silver flying saucer. The size and domed top of *Le Plateau* called up images of Michael Rennie emerging from his silver starship in *The Day the Earth Stood Still*. The colossus zoomed over the turning heads of my fellow gastronomic voyagers. It sailed in for a landing on the metal frame, where it was brought to rest gracefully as a second waiter placed bread, butter, mayonnaise, and vinegar on the table in the shadow of the unidentified flying platter.

I heard Rennie's voice whisper from the behemoth, "Klaatu barada nikto!"

The desire to immediately tear into *Les Fruits de Mer* in the middle of the Latin Quarter conflicted with a basic survival instinct telling me to figure out what the waiter served before I started to eat it.

"Good, monsieur?"

"*Bon, merci*," I answered, looking around the room to see how anyone else who had ordered *Le Plateau* was going about digging into it. Glancing to the far end, I saw another silver saucer being picked through without any particular formality.

I studied my *Plateau* rising from the broad surface of a half-foot Alp of crushed ice: all over was scattered an aquarium of sea life. The overall effect combined the random quality of the ocean washing shells up on the beach with the practiced hand of a master chef having perfectly cooked, cooled, opened, cut, and collated the most divergent specimens of cold seafood the ocean offered. It was huge.

I began to wade into the objects that were the most familiar. The oysters flinched as I forked a lemon and squirted juice on them. A large crab, cut in two, perched on the summit. Picking it apart felt like a science lab project. I moved from one picarooned piece to another, over shells, around claws, exploring unfamiliar meaty chasms. Occasionally the waiter would check back as though standing watch over amateur phrenologists fingertipping suspicious skulls.

The most peculiar thing in the assortment was a set of sea snails. I had never seen these types of snails outside a dentist's office goldfish bowl and didn't know they were edible—or that I would be ever offered the opportunity to eat one—bold stripes and delicate cone shapes made them almost too pretty. The hard part was getting the gastropod out of its shell. They had a small opening at the base of the shell a fork couldn't penetrate. The clever Procope provided a cork studded with pin-size spikes for unscrewing the snails, which were chewy and as tasty as the eraser on the end of a number-two pencil.

Halfway through *Le Plateau,* dinner arrived for the couple at the next table. The young blond man with sculpted Spock sideburns was seated so close we bumped elbows. He eagerly scooped the long, shallow center out of two containers that looked like lengths of beige garden hose split the long way. Each was about ten inches long and appeared, at second glance, as though it might be a breadstick with a strip of caramel filling down the middle. I kept gawking at these things. The pile of exotic sea creatures above my table looked tame compared to this... this... bone marrow! The man excavated grilled marrow from a cow's thighbone, scooping it like yogurt, eating it like so much oatmeal.

"Marrow," he said in polite English after noticing my psychotic expression. He was far too happy to explain every nuance of his experience. "The bone marrow is very dense, very thick. It must be eaten slowly, with much salt. That lightens it, makes it better. You know what I mean?"

"Salt?"

He took the shaker, letting it pour over a spoonful of gritty marrow. "It cuts it. Very necessary, I think, so that it does not fill you up. Always salt your marrow."

The man's girlfriend, three-loop art nouveau earrings dangling, looked longingly across the table at him. Her addled expression might have been reserved, in ancient times, for the face of a gladiator's mistress after he'd bloodied a coliseum of challengers.

"*Bien.*" He rested his spoon on the plate with the exhausted bones, and the marrow-eater turned his attention to the waiter standing attentively by his side. A dish for his second course was lowered so he could see a hump of raw ground meat oozing crimson, and beside it, little heaps of chopped onions, salt, pepper, capers, anchovies, parsley, and a cup with the meat of a raw egg.

"*Le steak tartare a votre facon.*" The waiter allowed the fellow to consider his next manly undertaking. The diner made a twirling motion with his fingers, and the waiter smiled and made a twirling motion back. He was moving from marrow to raw meat in a single leap. It alarmed me to think what might be next. Hooves? Tail? Poached udder? Stand back for the cart bearing the ox!

Soon the waiter returned with the ingredients mixed into a large red ball of meat and set it before the Parisian—his girlfriend approvingly watched him devour the feast. How was he ever going to burn up all those calories? Or slough off the cholesterol?

Consuming *Le Plateau* changed my conception of what things from the oceans could be served and how. When I returned home, everyone wanted to know what I had eaten in Paris. They asked for details frequently enough that my curiosity got the better of me, and I wrote Le Procope and received a nice note in return with this explanation.

Le Plateau Procope

Composition en Français (Ingredients in English)

- ✓ 16 Creuses de Bretagne Moyennes (16 oysters)

- ✓ 12 Moules d'Espagne (12 Spanish mussels)

- ✓ 12 Amandes Moyennes (12 medium almond-shaped snails)

- ✓ 2 Étrilles (2 velvet swimming crabs)

- ✓ 2 Clams (2 clams)

- ✓ 1 Coquille Bulots (125g) (1 whelk)

- ✓ 1 Coquille Vignots (125g) (1 periwinkle)

- ✓ 1 Coquille Crevettes Grises (50g) (1 gray shrimp)

- ✓ 4 Pieces Crevettes Roses (4 pink shrimp)

- ✓ 4 Demi-Citrons (4 half lemons)

- ✓ 1 Tourteau (500g) coupe en 2 (1 large crab cut in half)

- ✓ Mise en place pour 2 (Set for two people)

- ✓ Ramequin Vinaigrette Echalotes (shallot vinegar)

- ✓ 8 Tranches de Seigle (8 pieces of rye bread)

- ✓ 4 rondelles de Beurre Demi-Sel (4 pieces of lightly salted butter)

- ✓ 1 Ramequin Mayonnaise (mayonnaise)

- ✓ Rince-Doigts (finger bowl)

Servi sur grand Plateau, avec algues et glace pilée. (Serve on a huge platter piled with ice in the shape of a pyramid.)

1 *bouchon couvert d'aluminium* (an aluminum-covered cork) with four *piqued les pingles* (spikes for pulling the snails out of their shells)

February

The Observable Universe

THE ROUTINE FOR arranging the gourmet dinners got easier each month. I had debugged the process so a quick, funky invitation would go out. The participants filled in the blanks with the names of the dishes they would like to prepare, and I followed up with phone calls, when needed, to assemble the menu.

I can't remember who picked the Rio theme. We all did, I suppose, because we needed to hit a new continent, and in the middle of a gray winter, thinking about all that Brazilian sunshine sounded pretty good.

Invitation to Razzle Dazzle Rio

It's that happy time again. Ready for another in the continuous stream of joyous Sorensen Gourmet Dinners.

This time we wing our way down south to Rio, stopping at some of the fun spots in Brazil. Think of Manaus, Sao Paulo, Belo Horizonte, and the capital, Brasilia. Then smell the aroma of Brazilian gourmet cooking in the fine tradition of all Sorensen Gourmet Dinners.

On the table you may see: Brazilian beef, black bean soup, Ipanema onion soup, *xinxim de galinha* (chicken + shrimp and peanut + coconut sauce), really dark coffee, garlic and shrimp stew with coconut milk, coconuts, okra, palm oil (called *dende*), avocados, papaya, palm hearts, and melon. You may also find Amazon jungle puddings, roast stuffed suckling pig (we'll get a couple people together on this one), *feijoada completa* (pork and black beans, which are served every Saturday), and acai, a purple pulp of the Amazonian fruit thickened with puffed tapioca.

Now, this grand event will take place:

February 2 at 6 p.m. (except for Jay,
who will arrive at 5:30 p.m.)

YOUR RESPONSIBILITY:

To fill out the questionnaire and return. If it is not received very soon, you run the risk of not being included. Space is limited.

Enter the name of at least two suggested dishes you will prepare in grand gourmet style and bring to BRAZIL - The Sorensen Gourmet Dinners.

Yes—I will be drinking wine.
I will pay the Cellar Master approximately $18 per person.
As you know, the Cellar Master will select wines for the din-
ner that fully complement the cuisine.
OR
No—I will not be drinking wine.
Instead, I will be drinking the exotic Brazilian non-alcoholic
drinks, provided as part of the meal.

My name is: _____

I will be
coming with: _____

My phone
numbers are: _____ and_____.

My first and second
choices are: _____

Appetizer: _____

Entrée one: _____

Salad: _____

Soup: _____

Entrée the other: _____

Bread: _____

Dessert: _____

Brazil

MY DRIVE TO get a grounding in the cuisine of Rio led me to magazine articles and books about South America. These oozed thick suntan lotion from their slick articles and travel ads. The usual images were: sanitized beaches of sugar-white sand, blazing sun, dark oiled skin, long, perfect legs emerging from flawlessly white swimsuits, yellow straw hats, wide-striped cabanas, and uniformed waiters holding trays of turquoise drinks with little umbrellas. Despite these pictures, I did not believe most Brazilians were engaged in lying on the beach on a regular basis, and there was precious little information about what they ate.

To learn firsthand about their cooking and to get tips on how to stage a dinner true to the spirit of Rio, I called the Brazilian Consulate in New York. A woman answered in Portuguese—promising. For sure, this native would be proud to tell me about the gastronomic treasures of her native land.

"What do you want? Food?" she cried as though I had disrupted a major diplomatic negotiation.

"Is there someone there who could tell me what would constitute a proper night in Rio?" I asked.

"No!" she announced. I understood that South Americans—like Italians, Iberians, and other sun-soaked peoples—eat a small breakfast, work a while, break for a monster lunch until about 4:30, then trundle back to work briefly before going home for a little tune-up dinner. The consulate receptionist, suffering, I suppose, from low blood sugar because I had called before her gigantic lunch, ordered me to contact her national tourist office, which I did. The woman who answered the phone couldn't quite get into the spirit of me having a Brazilian gourmet dinner way out on the Minnesota prairie either. She sent a tourist packet full of pictures of waterfalls and more umbrella-dotted beaches, and no mention of food.

I turned to local sources, asking around for firsthand advice on Rio, and heard back from several people who had visited that part of the world. Plenty of people had been down there. Still, nobody said anything about the food. All their stories involved getting robbed. Many told me the only way to avoid having something stolen from you in Brazil was to go naked. To top this, one couple said they actually had their clothes stolen when they had taken them off to get some sun on Ipanema Beach.

Could we arrange our Brazilian dinner so people would be robbed between each course for authenticity?

The gourmet dinner, Razzle Dazzle Rio, should have produced a boisterous evening of open-toed shoes, Desi Arnaz "Babalú" shirts, and dancing with fruit on our heads. Yes, Desi was Cuban, but it was sort of the same thing that evening. The menu read raucously enough, and I expected a South American amusement park to break out. Oddly, the dinner turned academic. As much of the food was unfamiliar, we analyzed rather than enjoyed it. *Acarajé*—bean fritters spread over the plate like soft asphalt shingles—overcooked from lack of experience. *Ipanema sopa de feijão preto*, made of black beans and onions, smelled good, while no-neck chicken left a lemony aftertaste. Scallops in peanut and coconut sauce complemented a fluffy curried rice salad in a con-strained fashion. Overall, it seemed very foreign without being even slightly exotic, although I was able to assist in preparing several of the dishes.

The most spectacular recipe to come out of the evening requires care not to break the fish into pieces when moving the ingredients around. I liked the unstable aspect to creating it and the concentration required in joining the parts together. Jay came up with it.

Brazilian Scoundrel Red Snapper
with Coconut-Lime Sauce

Serves 6

- ✓ 6 6-ounce red snapper filets
- ✓ Butter to coat pan
- ✓ 1 cup bottled clam juice
- ✓ ¼ cup fresh lime juice
- ✓ 1 medium-size yellow onion, chopped
- ✓ Salt and pepper
- ✓ 1 10-ounce can whole tomatoes, drained and chopped
- ✓ ½ cup green peppers, chopped
- ✓ 3 tablespoons butter
- ✓ 3 tablespoons flour
- ✓ 1 cup coconut milk
- ✓ 2 tablespoons fresh cilantro, chopped
- ✓ 1 teaspoon ground cumin
- ✓ Poaching paper

Rinse filets and pat dry. Select a sauté pan large enough to fit the filets, and lightly coat the pan with butter. Arrange fish in pan and pour in clam and lime juices. Sprinkle chopped onion into liquid around fish. Sprinkle with salt and a grating of pepper.

Over medium heat, bring liquid to boil, reduce, and cover pan with a circle of poaching paper just a bit smaller than the pan. Continue to simmer 8 minutes.

Carefully(!) remove fish to platter and keep warm. Add tomatoes and green peppers to poaching liquid and bring to a boil. Cook, stirring until liquid is reduced by half. Strain liquid, reserving both liquid and vegetables, and wipe the sauté pan dry.

Add 3 tablespoons of butter to pan and melt over medium-low heat. Add flour and stir until thickened. Add coconut milk and reserved liquid from fish. Stir enough to blend. Increase heat to medium and cook, stirring constantly until smooth and thickened. *Do not boil!* For heaven's sake, pay attention.

Reduce heat to low, add cilantro, cumin, and reserved vegetables. Cook 2 to 3 minutes, stirring. Place fish into sauce with enormous care and simmer to warm through. Remove fish and place on serving platter and pour the sauce over fish.

An Unreliable Form of Conveyance

THE ONLY BLIP in the otherwise smooth and uneventful evening occurred when Bjorn's new car crapped out on the way home. He drove two blocks, and his Chevrolet simply stopped because of the cold weather.

Bam bam bam on my door. Bjorn came storming into the house, nostrils flaring, flames shooting out of his ears, red snapper on his breath. Lucretia trailed after him, her expression a combination of embarrassment and self-restraint.

"Goddamn car! Brand new!" Bjorn screamed. "I'm going to call somebody, wake somebody up. What the hell was the name of that dealership? They're going to do something about this right now!"

"I don't think anybody at GM is going to be very interested in your problem at this hour. I have enough trouble with car dealers in the daytime," I lamely offered, realizing he'd left his brain out on the snowy street. "It's after one o'clock in the morning."

"I don't care. I'm going to wake up the chairman of the board at General Motors if I have to!" he thundered and made several calls to phones nobody answered. He even tried to pull numbers in Detroit area codes, searching for the culprit responsible for his troubles. After he exhausted every number he could find, his adrenaline burned off, and I drove them home. Bjorn steamed in the passenger seat, refusing to wear his seat belt, while Lucretia, seated in the back, hopelessly tried to make small talk. She'd outdone everyone in the otherwise dull wardrobe department again with a Carmen Miranda-went-to-Rio ensemble that looked awkward sticking out from under her overcoat.

The great fun of these gourmet events came in seeing what sort of bizarre behavior people would put themselves and others through.

Two Gentlemen Want to Cook You Dinner

TOO OFTEN I scrambled around at the last minute without finding anyone to invite as my guest. Finding a date to invite to these dinners was not as easy as one might have hoped. I tried to locate eligible companionship through singles apps that either matched you up or allowed you to create profiles that sounded like this:

> Raconteur
> Likes walks around the lakes, cozy fires, good books, cross-country skiing. Values meaningful talks, summer fun, cinema. Thirty-something. Some muscle definition preferred.

I knew that sort of copy would not attract anyone I would get along with. As a response, I ran the following:

> Incredibly Ugly
> Never shower, stupid, unemployable, poor dresser, bankrupt, social derelict, embarrassing to be with, never exercise, politically incorrect, dull, boring, several severe behavioral problems, multiple disorders. Thirties. Save me.

I figured if the woman of my dreams didn't have a sense of humor, she wasn't going to get the put-on. Unfortunately, I got several responses—all from women who didn't shower, were embarrassing to be with, and had severe disorders similar to the ones mentioned in my ad. So much for reverse psychology. I let time pass and put out more of these, hoping for at least someone to invite to the dinners. A couple more of my efforts were very routine, but the last was significantly more sophisticated—I thought—and aimed at the thinking woman who could use her dictionary.

Opsimath

Man oh man, am I tired or what of dating grindingly apo-
retical, palinoian women! Where are the lively, alert, ram-
bunctious ladies supposedly looking for a prosperous,
offbeat guy? Tracy and Hepburn were older when they
met. Seeking similar romantic spark with emotionally sta-
ble, career-secure, animated, adventurous paramour
ready to get serious after years of churning the waters. If
you differentiate Schwarzenegger from Shakespeare,
baklava from balaclava—or would at least bother to
look it up if you heard the terms in polite company—prefer Katmandu to Duluth, sailing to powerboats, possess
verbal acuity, maliciously keen Vonnegutian insight to help
us both survive an increasingly exasperating world, do not
hesitate!

This approach resulted in some convoluted responses that divided
themselves into two groups: those who thought I was totally serious and
actually talked like this, and those who got the timbre but felt they had
to analyze everything in it. I thought this through and decided one of
the things that was missing in this approach—and dates—was a common interest, which would expand our horizons rather than limit them.
What about food?

The more I thought about it, the more I wondered if my gourmet
cooking skills could be a flight deck to launch a budding romance, or at
least get me a date for the dinners. I called up Patrick and pitched the
idea of joining forces.

"We'll offer to cook dinner for a couple of dates. Pick a menu, bottle
of wine, buy a baguette..."

"Yeah," Patrick said insightfully. "Women are more likely to respond
in pairs—at least the ones afraid to answer on their own."

"We can run a personal that talks about gourmet cooks. Something about looking for two women to eat dinner with us. We'll say something about good conversation."

"Yeah, OK, I'll do it, all right," Patrick said. "Let me know when you run it"

During my gastronomic learning period, I always felt everyone must be a better cook than me. It wasn't until I had been exposed to the widest variety of cooking that I really knew I could navigate my way around the kitchen better than most of my contemporaries. Not that I'm any grand chef, it's just that I had developed the confidence to wade into the kitchen with the certainty that a significant portion of what I prepared would be good. I felt that I had come far enough in this transformation to adapt it to romance with modest confidence.

I worried over what to put into this dinner offer, trying to put myself in the position of two women who were also tired of the dating scene. Perhaps we'd attract the attention of the pair who were new to all this and were looking for a safe opportunity to go with a girlfriend to take on a new challenge. The finished post read:

We Want to Cook You Dinner

Two gourmet cooks will prepare and serve two women—who come together or apply separately—a five-course repast. Excellent service and superior food prepared with our stunning capabilities. Fine wine. If you're convivial, lively conversationalists. Charming company. We'll make you glad you answered our ad.

On a quick read-through, the part that says we're going to prepare and serve two women sounds a little cannibalistic, but I figured they would know what we meant. Patrick and I posted it.

Four responses came, each written by two woman who were intrigued by the opportunity to eat for free and enjoy a gourmet dinner—at least that is what they wrote. The term *gourmet* in this case didn't mean the same thing to all contestants. It scared the first pair. Patrick called them to find they weren't comfortable having us cook for them right away and wanted to see what we were like in person before committing to eating something we cooked. They wanted to meet us at a bar to "talk a little and see who you are."

It was just as well. They weren't particularly interested in cooking, and Patrick was so nervous about meeting them that he made a big deal about the bar having raw oysters. His Oort kicked up, and he started grumbling as he ordered two dozen oysters and ate them all himself while we watched.

The second pair of responders appeared a little more promising as they agreed to come over for dinner and let us cook. Something seemed a little fishy about them on the phone. They asked what we'd be drinking and wanted some credentials, including where we worked and why we were so interested in cooking. We arranged for this dinner at my house, and once again, the closer we got to the date, the more skittish and uncooperative Patrick became. He turned into the Oort Man.

"If they're bad news, I mean, if we've made a mistake having them over here, we'll just get drunk so we won't notice," Patrick said. "We'll just hit the wine really early and blot them out."

I nodded as the doorbell rang. "They're here."

We greeted them, and I took their coats. As usual, there was a tall one and a short one, one a little prettier than the other. One more outgoing, happier, smarter, one who couldn't stand still.

Patrick took a look and headed into the kitchen. Their backs were to him, and I could see Patrick over their shoulders. He performed a broad pantomime, opening the refrigerator door, taking the large bottle of wine out, pointing to the wine, and then to his open mouth. Wine, mouth, wine, mouth—the signal to start blotting.

They turned out to be from the local fundamentalist Bible college, a school that made its students sign agreements not to drink, dance, or fornicate, or they would suffer expulsion—and probably eternal damnation. Patrick and I took the challenge to end their academic and religious careers on every possible count. Unfortunately, the two women had only a little wine. We served skewered sole with herb butter and a breadcrumb coating, accompanied by baked eggplant with rosemary and plenty of garlic. After dinner, the tall one played piano like a wizard. She could sight-read anything, and we sang with her accompaniment. But, as they say, nothing happened.

The third pair of eligibles turned out to be very nice. Both were nurses and had administrative jobs in pediatric units. Patrick and I prepared *Crevettes Sautés au Citron*—shrimp sautéed in lemon with garlic, olive oil, and a dash of soy sauce. We lightly steamed fresh carrots and accompanied this with bottles of an Oregon pinot noir. The most fascinating topic of conversation was one of them telling in detail how the other slept fourteen hours a day. She went on with stories about trying to wake up her roommate by jumping on her bed after the first twelve hours of snooze time. Patrick went on a couple of dates with the oversleeper but never roused enough interest to keep her from dozing off.

We called the fourth pair of women who responded and arranged to meet. Unfortunately, this final dinner was doomed from the beginning. The written response we'd received from these two read, "We aren't as old as you, but if we're too young, you're too old."

"Fighting words!" I said. "They have a lot of audacity, telling us we're too old."

"They're probably bad news, writing something like that to rile us up. We should skip them. Don't take the bait," Patrick said.

"They're the last ones who replied. It's them or nobody."

"Yeah, you're right, we might as well. It's only going to cost us dinner. That's not so bad, really, when you think about it. We get to eat."

It did turn out to be all that bad. It was Patrick's turn to have the dinner at his house, and he insisted on scheduling the dates to come over at eight o'clock. Pretty damn late. I tried several times to have him schedule it earlier, to get some idle chitchat out of the way before dinner, to take advantage of some getting-to-know-you time before eating. Patrick would have none of it.

"Eight o'clock," he insisted, and it was his house and his turn to host the thing, and he had that Oort clouding around his head. So I blame him entirely for what happened.

At eight on the dot, two women who were a little younger than we deserved or needed knocked on the front door. The tall one was a bleached blonde and thin. She wobbled, guided herself up the steps by holding onto the handrail, and steadied herself on the wall in the living room. She was a nurse. Her friend was an accountant who worked at some bean-counting job with the state.

Patrick and I prepared *Pot-au-feu*, the classic French boiled beef and vegetable dish with an herb bouquet, leeks, several large onions, and a garnish of freshly sliced turnips and parsnips. We opened bottles of a solid chardonnay.

It turned out the nurse had arrived drunk, and given her slight physique, it wasn't hard to see how a couple drinks would have knocked her on her butt. The two young ladies had killed several hours at a bar, waiting for Patrick's eight-o'clock start time.

When we weren't watching, the nurse groped her way up the stairs and quietly ralphed on the bathroom floor. Mission accomplished, she crawled down the hall and climbed into Patrick's bed, like an old college roommate come to spend a long weekend. This was not welcome news, nor a fitting finale, to our ambitious plan of offering gourmet dinners as a romantic come-on. The evening ended with the bean-counter cleaning the bathroom before guiding her staggering girlfriend out to the car. The sick nurse tried to make some final cute remarks as she stumbled out the front door.

Patrick and I skulked over to a local tavern to talk all this over, trying to convince ourselves we weren't fated for a life of endless catastrophes.

"It wasn't our cooking that caused it, Patrick," I said, reassuring the both of us. "It wasn't our cooking."

March

Let's Do the Mash

FOR MARCH, AFTER the uneventful Rio event, the gourmets decided on an evening of Bavarian cooking. Bavaria turned out to be the most awful, boring mess of any of the dinners, with only one simple recipe standing out. During the course of planning the menu, the gourmet opportunity appeared to hold special promise. We moved back to Europe, and the cold weather seemed perfect for hearty dishes such as a cheese-stuffed pasta, breaded veal, herring, spätzle, sauerkraut, Black Forest torte, and mashed potatoes.

Fortunately, when I decided to make real mashers for the dinner, I forgot about Patrick—who was hosting the dinner at his little house and acting as if it were the greatest intrusion he'd ever had to contend with—and concentrated on finding out more about the potato. Once I got into researching mashed potatoes, I found I didn't know anywhere near as much about this staple as I thought I did.

The potato is a contribution from the New World to the Old, and each region that has encountered it has interpreted the spud differently. Different societies boil, fry, or bake the potato and mix in inventive ingredients. Americans chow down four times more potatoes than any other vegetable, and it's on more menus than anything else—even hamburgers.

The scouting party of Gonzalo Jimenez de Quesada's foray through the Andes provided one of the earliest records of the potato's encounter with Europeans. His 1537 excursion into Incan territory probably first identified it, and the Spanish monk Hieronymus Cardano very likely conducted it to Spain. Pizarro also lays claim to liberating the potato from the Americas during his earlier 1534 exploration of Peru. In any case, it's neither Sir Frances Drake nor Sir Walter Raleigh who deserve credit for the find, though they're often mentioned in this regard.

Unfortunately, restaurants seldom serve authentic mashed potatoes, relying instead on instant, dehydrated flakes that come in boxes like cereal. Instant potatoes either have the consistency of a chalky paste or are diluted into a thin soup that might as well be served in a glass so you can drink it. Even McDonald's had long switched from fresh to frozen fries, eliminating the only reason for going there. I remember insisting my parents take a five-mile diversion to McDonald's because of the fresh potato fries they served when I was a kid. If they started offering fresh potato French fries again, they could charge a premium for them.

After careful observation, I came to believe the prime stumbling block to using real potatoes in most restaurants is the skin. It is my deeply held belief that the way to get around the issue of skins is to leave them on. Peeling potatoes is classic drudgery. Laurel and Hardy movies show the guys sitting at the foot of a mountain of potatoes, peeling them one at a time as punishment—and for good reason. Potatoes are difficult to peel. No device for peeling them has yet been invented that can easily separate the skin from the inside, even though thousands more implements have been invented for processing potatoes than for all other fruits and vegetables combined. Only burned-out tradition creates the compulsion to clean the potato by removing its skin. I believe there is no reason for this. The potato skin is an edible wrapper full of vitamins and minerals, with a taste of the dirt from the place they grew.

Looking at the big picture, the potato is the swelled, underground stem end of the plant called a *tuber*. These tubers come in an endless marshaling of standard and exotic varieties. There are early, new, waxy, baking, main crop, and other categories that overlap and have different names for the same things. Potatoes come in many colors, notably yellow, brown, red, purple, white, and blue. All grocery stores stock russet potatoes, which we use as a multipurpose staple. They're named for their russet color. There are also hundreds more, including Spunta, Apollo, Bea, Yukon Gold, Ostara, Resy, Dirtema, Ulster, Sceptre, Maris Bard, King Edward, Ramano, and Duke of York.

I found I could mash any of these and only needed to experiment to discover which I preferred. However, there is a test to determine the best mashers, described in Harold McGee's superlative book *On Food and Cooking*. This volume takes a scientific approach to cooking, challenging conventional notions of kitchen lore. McGee divides potatoes into mealy and waxy types. The mealy are best for mashing as their cells separate when cooked. Waxy potatoes stick together, making them better for fries, scallops, and potato salads. The test for selecting the best mashers is essentially floating the potatoes in salty water. The mealy potatoes sink because they're denser. These are the ones to mash.

I mash about anything and, after tons of experimentation, believe that skin-on mashers are the way to go. This straightforward recipe, developed from its start at the Bavarian Gourmet Dinner, has been received with great acclaim ever since.

Skin-on Mashers

To serve four people, scrub the skins of 6 medium-size potatoes with a wire brush to get the dirt off. Dig out any eyes and bruises that look too big to smash. Cut the potatoes into four or five pieces each. In a saucepan, cover potatoes with water and bring to a boil. Simmer about 25 minutes, or until you can stick a fork into them with impunity. No salt is needed. I always try to cut down the amount of salt in things, but it's up to the chef.

Drain the pot and leave the potatoes in the bottom as you add 6 teaspoons of butter, margarine, olive oil or whatever the health researchers announce will not clog your arteries this week, and ½ cup of milk or light cream. Skim milk works fine. There's no need to heat up the milk before you put it in to keep the potatoes from cooling down too much. Usually they're hot enough, and the heat of the pot will keep things hot anyway.

Smash the potatoes to mix the ingredients. There are dedicated potato mashers, but if you've cooked the potatoes enough, they'll mash easily with a whisk. You don't need to show people how hard you're working by clanking a masher around the pot to make a lot of noise.

The skins will mix in, and you should not have any lumping problems, which occur when the potatoes aren't cooked enough. However, leaving in a few lumps is a great way to demonstrate authenticity.

Add a little ground nutmeg. You can also add ⅓ cup applesauce or 1 cup chopped scallions or 1 cup chopped parsley, but add only one extra ingredient to the same batch. When it comes to adding a bunch of other stuff to the mashers, keep your hands to yourself!

And when you serve them, explain that the skins are good for people and that your guests should appreciate your mashed potatoes much more than other potatoes because the skins are mixed in there.

As you slide them onto the table, say, "Eat these mashers. They're good for you."

Mention Bavaria and everybody thinks of Munich and the Alps, beer, wild-game hunting, sauerkraut and sausage, meat, meat, meat, dumplings, mountains, forests, and whipped cream. I checked my favorite bookstore for German cookbooks. They had thousands of particulars on Italian and French cuisine, hundreds on British, and even three on the food of Scotland. There was only one tiny book about German cooking. It was small, cute, and useless.

Upon investigating other sources, I did come up with some of the distinctions between cooking styles in Germany. In the north, where it's cool, the influences of Denmark, Poland, and Holland are felt, so they go for hearty soups and fish. The central region is more apt to offer breads, vegetables, and ragouts. In the Rhineland, meals are lighter, while Bavaria eats heavy-duty: meat and whipped cream. The dish named for the region—Bavarian Cream—is itself a cold, rich dessert made with egg custard.

We waded into this gourmet dinner without much concern for what was authentically Bavarian and what slopped over into other styles of German cooking. It was the most haphazard gathering we'd had, and considering the outcome, we probably shouldn't have done Bavarian at all.

Hosting our Bavarian dinner was too much for Patrick's Oort. Nothing was right. Everything inconvenienced him. As the Cellar Master, he got lazy and picked lousy beer and a thin Rhine wine, then made excuses for them. He mumbled some disobliging justifications for his beverage choices and dragged us into a malaise. The weather added zero-temperature readings and plenty of snow, further spiraling us into failure.

Mix Your Mustard Daily

GOOD MUSTARD IS an essential part of the Bavarian experience.

Illuminating gastronomic experiences came in unexpected ways and in places I never would have suspected. I'd always wanted to visit New

Zealand, as I wondered why people kept talking about it being such an amazing place with an interesting food scene.

The most efficient way to tour New Zealand is in a caravan, the Kiwi version of a mini motorhome. It comfortably slept me and the two friends I brought along and rode well. We picked up the vehicle in Christchurch, on the South Island, and headed south.

Most of the trip we stayed in caravan camps, though we managed two nights as guests of Mern and Nathlie McLean, who operated a bed-and-breakfast on their Caroline Valley farm near Dipton. We discovered their roomy farmhouse beside a road off the main highway. It was square and white with a spacious garden and some fruit trees scattered around the yard. Heading up the driveway, we were greeted by their four sheepherding dogs barking from wooden kennels: Ming, Chin Chin, Corkey, and Jen. Nathlie appeared with an amused expression, anticipating the usual odd behavior from Americans, and directed us to park the caravan around the back of the house.

In the middle of the kitchen, her husband, Mern, stood in his under-shirt shaving with an electric razor, adding to the homey quality. This demonstrated the relaxed, accepting nature of New Zealanders as well as anything during our trip.

Nathlie motioned for us to check out the bedrooms. "Come upstairs, let me show you your kit. Yes, all right then? Eh, you be ready for supper 'bout half past six?"

"Yes, ma'am," we said quite automatically, and at half past six, we were back downstairs at the large dining room table. Mern and Nathlie sat at each end with the three of us spaced out between them. The house had a hospitable spareness, with a few pictures and a couple comfortable chairs. We recounted our trip and received advice about where next to go and the best things to do once we got there.

The meal, included in the farm-stay package, was a solid repast of roasted potatoes and beef with a small ceramic pot of mustard on the table. In America, people usually only put a jar of mustard out if hot dogs are the main course. I didn't even recognize what was in the small cup as mustard at first, thinking it was some yellow mayonnaise or an unfamiliar sauce.

"That's Colman's powdered mustard. We mix it with milk rather than water. It's quite good," Mern said, dabbing a knifeful onto his plate.

"We think it's hotter mixed with milk," Nathlie added as she passed it to me.

I had seen mustard seed whole, but never ground into powder—more evidence of my cultural deprivation.

"Could I see it?"

"Of course," Mern said, getting the container from the kitchen.

Colman's Double Superfine Mustard comes in a bright yellow box with red lettering that I was quite taken by. There's a drawing of a cow and a royal seal with notification that this mustard is manufactured by appointment of Her Majesty Queen Elizabeth II. On the back are some pictures of medals from the 1878 Paris Exhibition and the story of Colman's two hundred years of growing, milling, and blending mustard around the world. I like the authority that royal emblems and prizes from competitions give food boxes. In the directions, Colman's insists: Always mix your mustard daily.

But we were eating the mustard with beef! I thought New Zealand was all about sheep. Mern had one of the most prime breeding bulls in the entire country, he thought, and sold the stud services of his prize Santa Gertrudis, "which all Americans should be familiar with," he insisted, "since the breed was developed beginning in the early 1900s near Kingsville, Texas."

I had traveled all the way to New Zealand, was staying on 568 acres with a flock of 1,800 breeding ewes and 500 hoggets, and this turns out to be home to the prize bull in the entire country. I casually mentioned a sidelight of my gourmet obsession to Mern. "I want to shear a sheep."

He looked up from his plate of beef, his expression asking why anybody would want to shear, much less eat, sheep when there are so damn many of them. New Zealanders live and breathe sheep, smell them, walk through them, see them constantly, trip over the things. Why would I be interested?

"You want to shear a sheep?" Mern said politely, with a glint suggesting he understood the disorientation that comes with traveling across so many time zones. My companions hung their heads in embarrassment.

"Could I do it? I mean, do you shear them all year, or is it something that only happens in the spring or fall?"

Mern squinted at Nathlie, then at me. "You want to shear a sheep? Really?"

There was a great deal I didn't know about sheep, so I took this as an opportunity to start asking questions. One thing in particular puzzled me. When driving through the vast sheep ranges on our way down the South Island, we'd seen some sheep with colors on them. They'd have red or blue or green on their backs and tails and, in some cases, their heads.

"The ram is placed in the enclosure with the sheep at the time of year when they are to begin the reproduction cycle," Mern explained. "They're either in heat on their own, or the presence of the ram brings them into heat. So we can plan on which sheep will be giving birth at what time, we hang a bib over the ram's neck. The bib has a colored crayon in the front, and this marks the sheep when he serves her. We change the color of the crayon on different weeks so we can tell about when each sheep will deliver."

After we'd talked sheep for a while, Mern went on to share some of his perceptions of Americans. He had seen the movie *American Graffiti* and was impressed by the cruisin' the Americans had done in it and couldn't believe we'd spend our Saturday nights driving up and down the main street of a small town.

"You do things differently, things that would have never occurred to us in New Zealand," Mern said, happily bewildered.

"What did you do on Saturday night when you were a teenager? Did you get in the car and drive around?" I asked.

"Well, yes, we did, perhaps not in the same way. Not with the same—you know—fanfare. I'd get in a car with my friends, and we'd drive into town."

"And would you cruise up one side of the street and down the other?"

"No, about all we'd do is watch the lights come on, then turn around and come home. That was a Saturday night in Dipton, New Zealand."

Later that evening I helped Mern chase a gigantic sheep from a muddy field up a wooden ramp into a small barn.

"She'll dry off overnight in there. That'll make it easier for you tomorrow. I think we want to make it as easy as we can, don't you?"

"Oh, yes," I agreed.

The next day the sheep had dried out, and Mern took me back to the barn. It had a slat floor with several pens for sheep and bins for holding wool. He led me to a narrow pen holding my massive sheep in the corner.

"This'll be a good runty one here for you. I've singled her out for dog tucker."

"Dog tucker?"

"We feed the runty ones to the dogs. Dog tucker's all they're good for—too scrawny for anything else. She won't give you much of a fight."

"Of course not."

"You wanted a nice docile one now, didn't you?" he asked again.

The animal did not look all that small and passive to me. "Whatever you suggest. What do I need to know?"

Mern pointed out the finer details of the old shearing barn. There were three shearing stations with the shearing equipment's electric motor bolted to the heavy rafters with an articulated steel drive shaft coming off it. Three universal joints in the shaft allowed the sheep shearer complete flexibility in positioning the clippers. The power transferred to the clipper head fluidly, making a fluttering sound like a hedge trimmer. Mern demonstrated the mechanical shearer.

"Now an experienced fellow will shear up to three hundred sheep. They'll do anywhere between two and three hundred, depending."

"One man will shear three hundred sheep in a week?" I gasped.

"In an eight-hour day. We usually look for a fellow who can shear 275, at least. That's a good round number, isn't it?"

I figured if we're talking eight times sixty minutes, that is better than one sheep every two minutes, with no break for lunch. Mern had me step into a pair of overalls and led me into the pen where my sheep— soon to be dog tucker—nervously tried to escape.

"Just lead her into the shearing pen and turn her over on her back. You won't get any problems then." Mern showed a great deal of patience, nudging the sheep toward me with his knees. "Go ahead, just turn her over."

When you've never handled an animal other than a dog or cat, and you didn't grow up on a farm, handling a sheep is like wrestling an alien from Krypton. It made me realize again how far I had been separated from the animal world. As I seized the sheep and followed Mern's instructions to roll it onto its back, I was struck by its strength and determination. All this resistance from a species called *sheep*. The fight persisted until the sheep rolled over. The instant it went on its back, legs pointed in the air, the animal turned completely docile, entering a nearly catatonic state.

"I killed it?"

"No, you didn't. Now you take the clipper and shear." Mern guided me through the first few swipes. The clipper head moved smoothly, separating the wool from the underlying skin, turning the fluffy dirty-white beast into a skinny little pink animal that resembled a goat. I took a great deal of care and a lot of time, much slower than an experienced shearer.

When I finished, Mern asked if I wanted to see the rest of the process, where he cut the sheep's throat and took it apart for dog tucker. I declined. I wanted to get closer to my food, but not that close.

As I left, I noticed numbers and names and dates all along the shearing barn rafters. During the season, workers write the date and number of sheep they sheared and their name as a record. My last act in the shearing barn was to take an indelible marker and write on the rafter my name and the date and beside it a large numeral one—a permanent record of the total number of sheep I had sheared that day.

The last night at the McLeans' we were served corned lamb, probably because of the commotion I had made over the beef. Nathlie explained that they take their own meat to the local butcher, who soaks it in brine.

She suggested we try the same thing back home. The corned lamb can also be smoked, which she recommended we try as well.

The McLeans also roast lamb, with great success, for the visitors from many countries who stay with them. They're often asked for the recipe.

Mern & Nathlie's New Zealand Roast Lamb

Serves a whole bunch of people

Place lamb roast in a roasting pan. Combine the following ingredients; pour over lamb.

- ✓ 1 onion, chopped
- ✓ ½ cup honey
- ✓ ½ cup dried apricots, chopped
- ✓ 2 tablespoons beef stock
- ✓ 2 cups water
- ✓ 2 tablespoons lemon juice
- ✓ 2 tablespoons tomato sauce
- ✓ 1 tablespoon butter
- ✓ 1 teaspoon ginger
- ✓ 1 teaspoon curry powder
- ✓ Salt and pepper

Roast lamb at 375° for 30 minutes per pound or until internal temperature reaches 160° for rare and up to 180° for well-done.

Baste while roasting. Thicken juice with corn flour as needed.

April

Pan-Blackened Meals

WE CHOSE NEW Orleans for April because everybody thought they knew something about the true experience of the place. It would be lighter and more fun than the Bavarian quagmire, and people wanted to do something American.

Nothing said New Orleans like K-Paul's in the French Quarter. K-Paul's owner, Paul Prudhomme, was a gigantic man the shape of Wembley Stadium, with a thick black beard. He always wore a starched white chef's outfit with an A-bomb hat. His technique for cooking blackened redfish became such a success, it's been adopted as a New Orleans staple. Prudhomme's pan-blackened redfish caught on with such fervor, the government temporarily suspended fishing for redfish—a previously ignored species—so they could conduct a count to make sure it didn't become extinct.

Today there are all sorts of different pan-blackened fish, chicken, steak, and shrimp dishes on menus around the country.

I had been a Prudhomme fan for a long time and purchased several copies of his cookbook, but gave them all away for Christmas or wedding presents, so I didn't have one left for myself. Eventually I got down to New Orleans and made a pilgrimage to the French Quarter.

I didn't expect a Disneyland when I got there. I did, however, want more depth to the stores in such a deliberately touristy area. Every French Quarter shop sold porcelain masks, and the same T-shirts hung in all the windows as if a boatload of them had run aground at the city wharf and stores could find nothing else to offer.

The French Quarter is a rectangle, six blocks deep and thirteen blocks wide, adjoining the contemporary business district on the far side of downtown from the Superdome where the Saints play. It's largely a residential area, but there are plenty of bars with restaurants, bars with music, bars with bakeries, bars selling walk-around drinks, and other bar-oriented ventures. Parking is impossible. Finding a spot on the street is a land rush.

Hurricanes, high-octane fruit cocktails, are available to buy and drink while cruisin' the streets. There are men selling these big, tall drinks from open doorways and hole-in-the-wall joints on every block. I became curious if there was any difference between hurricanes, so I asked several of these outdoor bartenders how they made theirs. Each served a slightly different recipe for their bar's version of the famous drink, but none was decidedly different from the others.

Houses in the Quarter, which building codes strictly regulate, are compact. Most of them two or three stories tall to maintain the area's traditional skyline. Buildings can be anything—misbegotten combinations of Creole hideaways, Victorian mini-mansions, slave quarters, or Greek Revival facades with flower-strewn courtyards. The French Quarter really isn't built in a French style, of course. They're predominantly Spanish-style buildings, since the blistering fire of 1788 gutted the area and rebuilding took place under the Spanish administration of Charles III. France's Louis XV had been pitched out well before then.

Sadly, K-Paul's is gone now, though there are many other restaurants with fantastic menus to choose from.

Don't Mince Words

PREPARING FOR THE New Orleans gourmet dinner, I thought back over the restaurants I had visited around the country. I've rarely found anything called New Orleans cooking, but there was Cajun food on menus everywhere.

Cajuns live in Acadia, an area in southwestern Louisiana. The distinct heritage of this region is expressed in its art, customs, music, and food—especially the food.

The bayous of Cajun country were settled by the Spanish and French, though the Acadians were the first colonists to permanently establish themselves in the territory. These descendants of French farmers were booted from seventeenth-century Nova Scotia by the British. A few managed to survive the harsh transplant, and those rugged souls adapted their French colonialist, Canadian backwoods methods to a new environment. They incorporated the fauna and flora of Louisiana into their cooking, jumbling it together with Spanish themes to beget tenacious, pungent dishes that express the smashing together of unco-operative cultures.

Bjorn always wanted a final say in planning the gourmet dinners. Back home on the phone, he tested my knowledge of the cuisine.

"OK, then, Sorensen. We can have Cajun cooking at this New Orleans thing, but what about Creole? Aren't you going to make sure we have Creole represented too?"

Sometimes you just want to haul off and slug your dinner partners. "I'll bite, Bjorn. What's the difference between Cajun and Creole cooking?"

"In Creole they use three chickens to feed one family, and in Cajun they use one chicken to feed three families."

Give me a cute answer to something I really want to know, and I'll get to the truth at the bottom of it. What was the difference between these Louisiana cuisines?

Beginning in my own kitchen, I fled to my growing inventory of cookbooks, finding comments about one style or the other without the facts needed to compare them and understand their differences. Neither in the local public library nor in local bookstores could I find definitive answers to my questions. Instead, I called Paul Prudhomme, whose New Orleans number was on the label of one of his Louisiana Cajun Magic spice bottles on my shelf. When you want a straight answer, go to the source.

"The Chef," which is what the staff member who answered the phone called him, was "in Europe at a cooking show, but we'll leave him a message with your question." It surprised me that more people in New Orleans don't have southern accents. The mature, kind-sounding lady who fielded my call sounded like she might have been from Pittsburgh.

I was quite willing to wait for one of the most famous chefs in the universe to call me back with the definitive distinctions between Cajun and Creole cooking. Leaving a message did not bother me if it would eventually clear things up. About twenty minutes later the phone rang. Prudhomme's personal assistant was on the line. She was very polite and helpful, nearly breathless, it sounded, from scurrying around the office for a definition.

"Sir, to answer your inquiry, I have located several definitions of which I believe the Chef would approve."

"That's great," I said, not-so-secretly hoping it was the Chef himself calling back from Europe to fill me in personally. "I appreciate your help."

"Cajun is country cooking based on the French colonial peasants who were displaced to the Louisiana backcountry, whereas Creole is comparatively sophisticated city cooking out of New Orleans proper. It has more rich sauces. It's a result of the layering of influences from the British, Spanish, Indians, French, Africans, and others who lived here. One way each colonial administration added its tastes was by hiring lo-cal servants and cooks who picked up on the imported cooking styles. When the various administrations moved on, the chefs stayed behind, retaining the best of what they'd learned, adding it to the local cuisine. In a nutshell, that is the difference between these two Louisiana-born styles."

"That's a great explanation." I thanked her. "And if I could just leave my message for the Chef, I would sure like to hear from him directly."

"We'll see," she said. I never heard back.

The menu for the New Orleans Gourmet Dinner picked up a variety of tastes. We served, and I learned to make, oysters in bacon, cold smoked eggplant soup with hot pepper cream, Don't-Mince-Words Jambalaya, Cajun martinis, black bean soup, and pecan pie. There were some other odds and ends, but these were the most engaging of the rec-ipes.

Lucretia, I think, had the idea for Cajun martinis. "They can be hot—very hot," she warned. "I drank one down in New Orleans, and it nearly knocked me to the ground. I'm not sure how you make them, but I stumbled across them at a bar where people were having crayfish races out on the sidewalk."

On the night of the New Orleans dinner, there was an underlying consensus that the Cajun martini was a bad idea.

"I'm not drinking one of those. They put hot peppers in the bottle," Rex insisted. He'd been a little less aggressive since I spread word about the exact nature of his new business opportunity.

Enthusiasm for the martinis grew as Lucretia and Bjorn started sipping them. When Jay arrived—late as usual—wearing his gray-flecked wool camping socks and khaki pants, white hair and beard flowing in the breeze, he headed straight for them.

"Oh, hell, those little things. They ain't going to hurt nothing. I've been burned by a match worse that." Jay buoyantly gulped a small Cajun martini and examined the gin bottle, admiring the peppers in the bottom. "They get better the longer you let them sit down there," he said, setting an example for others to follow.

New Orleans Cajun Martini

Put a few fresh whole cayenne hot peppers into a decent bottle of gin and let them soak. Use little red peppers—fresh, not dried. Let them sit there several days. The Scoville heat units (SHU)—a measurement system developed by American pharmacist Wilbur Scoville—of the gin can be moderated by the number of peppers you put in the bottle and the number of ice cubes proportionate to the amount of gin in the glass when you drink it. Pour over ice and sip. You might try vermouth for fun, but it will probably be terribly overpowered.

As the smells of the food began to saturate my house, some of the more suspicious gourmets sipped a little from the Cajun martini bottle and liked it. Then they had some more. And by the end of the first entrée, a second bottle of Cajun martinis was opened, and the entire crowd gallantly started drinking. Once a person tried them, without fail, they had another and started unbuttoning their shirt.

The hit of the evening was a hot, grayish pot of jambalaya that Jay has made several times since, refining it every time. It's one of his favorites. After a second Cajun martini, he introduced the dish. "You've just got to come out and say what you're thinking when you're talking jambalaya. Don't mince words."

Don't-Mince-Words Jambalaya

Serves 8 or so

- ✓ 4 chicken breast halves, skin -on and bone -in
- ✓ 2 ounces salt pork, chopped
- ✓ 4 Italian sausages—or another spicy type—cut into inch-long pieces
- ✓ 1 large onion, chopped
- ✓ 1 cup celery, chopped
- ✓ 1 cup green peppers, chopped
- ✓ 2 cloves garlic, minced
- ✓ 2 16-ounce cans of plum tomatoes, drained and chopped
- ✓ 1-pound smoked ham, chopped
- ✓ 3 bay leaves
- ✓ 1½ teaspoons dried basil
- ✓ 1 teaspoon dried thyme
- ✓ 2 teaspoons cayenne pepper
- ✓ 2 teaspoons black pepper
- ✓ 1 tablespoon Tabasco
- ✓ 1 cup tomato sauce
- ✓ 1-pound medium-size shrimp, shelled and deveined

- ✓ 2 cups clam juice
- ✓ 3½ cups rice

In a large saucepan, cover chicken breast halves with water. Bring water to a boil; reduce heat and simmer about 10 minutes. Remove the breasts and cool. Remove skin and bones from chicken, returning skin and bones to poaching liquid, and bring to boil. Simmer 10 minutes more. Discard skin and bones, and reserve 2 cups of the broth for your Don't-Mince-Words Jambalaya. Cut chicken into 1-inch pieces and set aside.

In 6-quart saucepan, cook salt pork over medium heat until fat is rendered and hot. Add sausage and cook, turning until sausage begins to brown—about 4 or 5 minutes. Add onion, celery, and green pepper. Cook until all is tender, stirring about 4 or 5 minutes. Add a bit of butter or vegetable oil if needed.

Add garlic and cook another 2 minutes. Add tomatoes and cook another 2 minutes. Add tomato sauce, ham, bay leaves, basil, thyme, cayenne and black pepper, Tabasco, and the chicken pieces. Cook, stirring, another 2 minutes.

Add shrimp and cook 1 minute. Add clam juice and reserved chicken broth and bring to a boil.

Add rice and reduce heat to simmer. Cook, covered, stirring occasionally, 15 to 20 minutes to blend all ingredients. Add water if needed to keep jambalaya from drying out.

Serve, passing the Tabasco, and tell your guests, "Don't mince words."

All Gourmeted Out

UNFORTUNATELY, THE ADMINISTRATIVE challenges of the gourmet dinners were taking their toll on my zeal for single-handedly sustaining the group. I was getting gourmeted out. I had already learned gobs about cooking and felt confident preparing and ad-libbing my way through hundreds of dishes. However, at times it seemed all I heard were complaints. Bjorn and Patrick weren't hitting it off. No particular reason for this except for their in-your-face personalities. Lucretia traveled a lot for work, and there was friction between her and Bjorn. They'd been going to more counseling sessions. The only progress made amounted to Lucretia talking the counselor into convincing Bjorn to part his hair differently.

At the New Orleans dinner, Lucretia had grabbed Bjorn by the hand and dragged him across the dining room to me as the jambalaya was served.

"Doesn't he look better? Don't you think it helps? It really helps!" Lucretia told me.

I did not see much difference.

I began to realize how much complaining wore on me and that it was hard to keep focused on my original goal of learning to cook when I spent so much time organizing. If I really wanted to learn to cook rather than be a dinner organizer, I thought I might try some formal training at a swank cooking school. They'd give me an embossed certificate with five stars and an inscription in Latin on it—like the royal emblem on the mustard box—proof of my competence.

Finding just the right place for me to take a class wasn't easy until I got word about Cooks of Crocus Hill, an enlightened kitchen-supply store with its own cooking school. It is situated in a funky part of St. Paul, anchoring a cluster of shops in an area catering to the local crowd who truly want to live in Sedona and Mendocino and on the Cote d'Azur. Cooks occupies an old brick building with the classroom upstairs and the pots, pans, cookbooks, jars of capers, and various olive oils at ground level. I decided to take some classes there to augment my burgeoning skills and change my perspective on the greater gastronomic experience.

Cooks of Crocus Hill sends out a regular bulletin with two or three dozen classes stretched over three months. Most classes are one-evening events, about four hours with twelve to fifteen students and one instructor who is an expert in the field. A popular basic class, *How to Boil Water*, runs several sessions and is designed for people with even less culinary preparation than I had. Cooks advertised this popular class as one that "meets the needs of people who have never ventured into the kitchen to do any real cooking." It covers omelets, poached eggs, a simple cheese sauce, chicken salad, and meatloaf. At the time, it was taught by the school's director, Lois Lee.

Lois was a lot of fun. She radiated a warm confidence as both an experienced chef with expert credentials and an affable mentor. Her hair a comfortable salt-and-pepper, she carried herself with the undulating bloom of a grandmother who just finished baking cookies for a class of third-graders. She studied at La Varenne, Cordon Bleu, and L'Académie de Cuisine, which is in Maryland rather than anywhere else such a name might suggest. Her ability to remember names and faces was remarkable, and she managed all the students, teachers, and food with a relaxed intuition.

I began by enrolling in a few classes, spacing them out over some weeks, and selecting a variety of topics I found interesting. I took Turkish cooking and a class on soups. One went over preparation of fish and another of pasta. Both of these were subjects I had already learned enough about while organizing my own gourmet dinners that I didn't feel I got a lot out of them. After a few classes, I hesitated to take any more, not because of the quality of instruction, but because the students knew so little. I couldn't believe their lack of a simple grounding—or that I had learned so much on my own. They couldn't tell a clove of garlic from an entire head. Couples fought over the difference between chives and parsley. Soup burned. White sauce spilled. Directions were misread with disastrous results.

In some classes the teacher spent a lot of the time organizing the students into groups of three or four and assigning them tasks for the evening's menu. Other instructors—the more autocratic ones—prepared all the food themselves, talking all the time with the students seated at the long preparation table in front of them. These instructors knew it was much less trouble, and many fewer dishes to clean, if the students just watched. It made the event more like watching a slow-paced TV show.

One class stood out from all others. It was conducted by Eberhard Werthmann, head of a restaurant school in St. Paul. Born in Germany, he'd been an executive chef for thirty years. Eberhard presented himself as a thick-shouldered man with a pleasant intensity. All hands and forearms, he approached teaching with the energy of a master. Eberhard knew everything there was to know about cooking in a restaurant. He exuded the happy energy of a man secure in the kitchen, although he hadn't come to talk with us about food this evening.

Eberhard came to tell us about knives.

Cutting Up in Class

EBERHARD SAILED INTO class, shirtsleeves rolled to his elbows. He enthusiastically dumped a brown paper bag of fifty knives on the counter and spread them like a deck of cards. They came in all sizes, from stubby paring knives to long stilettos, along with specialty blades for outlandish kitchen tasks. It felt like we were scanning Dr. Frankenstein's surgical supplies, not just culinary weaponry.

"How many of you have knives you like in your own kitchen?" Eberhard asked jubilantly. No one raised a hand. "No?" he said. "I suppose that is why we are all here then, to learn more about the knife and how to use it. A good knife, kept sharp, will last you a long time, as it adds great pleasure to the hours you spend in the kitchen."

It turned out there was much more to the simple knife than I had ever imagined. Eberhard's hands moved fast as he quickly pointed out several details. If you look down the length of a knife, it should taper to a point. The cheap ones don't. The metal of the blade should come all the way back into the handle and be completely integrated so the metal is visible all the way around the handle's edge. Cheap knives don't use as much metal in the tang, so they wrap the handle around a shortened stub rather than fully sandwiching the metal between handle halves. Rivets should hold the handle together. Better knives build up the guard in front of your fingers too.

He also showed us specialty knives, though he insisted a master chef can get by using only a sturdy six inch French chef's knife. Eberhard could do everything with these, probably play ukulele with one if he wanted to. The French chef's knife came in different sizes, and by the time Eberhard finished showing us the tricks to slicing onions, mincing garlic without touching it, and cutting an apple to look like a chicken— we were all fans.

This was the only class I had been to that adjourned to a bar afterward to talk and talk about knives. When I ran into some of the class members later, we'd all thrown out our drawers of old knives and purchased new ones. If I had only one cooking class to take again, it would be a good class on knives.

May

Stealth Mushrooms

THE FIRST TIME I heard of morels, the legislature had voted them the Minnesota state mushroom. This made front-page news and told me more about my adopted state than a thousand historical society picnics. Turns out there is not only a myth, but an obsession over this pointy little sponge covered with crevices and whose colors run from yellow to brown to gray.

Because morels are considered by many to be the most delicious mushrooms in the world, several research labs have invested major venture capital trying to grow them commercially. All scientists found was that they can't yet cultivate morels with the taste, texture, and durability of those found in the wild—when they can even be found in the wild.

If anybody ever figures out how to grow good ones, there is plenty of retail potential. Morels are, ounce for ounce, one of the most expensive items in a grocery store. As a result, everybody who cooks has stories about trying to track them down in the wild. This has given the morel a myth-powered cult following. There are legends about the places morels grow and how to find them. When rumors spread that morels have been sighted, people disappear for days into the woods to search.

I decided to join the pursuit and checked with local mushroom cult devotees who confirmed, in exasperation, how unpredictable morels are. They all said the same thing: "You have to wait until just the right moment to find them. Then you run off and look in likely places, praying they will be there. If there's not enough rain, they skip a year. If you go too late, you miss them altogether." These sources assured me that as spring works its way north, the morels come with it, sprouting in a thin ripple—south to north—across the continent as the weather warms. Having such a long winter, we would be well into May before enough of a thaw cut loose any mushrooms in Minnesota.

Thinking about morels heightened my interest in mushrooms in general. I paid closer attention to them in stores and restaurants, and killed time waiting for spring by hunting for mushrooms on local restaurant menus. Many restaurants experiment with mushroom dishes. One of the more successful recipes I have run across appeared on the menu of a restaurant in Minneapolis.

It was one of the popular haunts at the edge of the Twin Cities university campus. It operated in the shell of an old transient hotel, stripped to its brick walls and refinished with new wood floors and buffalo heads. Ancient neon signs from defunct plumbing companies and grocery stores swung from the ceiling. I ordered the stuffed mushrooms off the appetizer menu, which were recommended by a member of the mushroom cult. A boat-shaped ovenproof dish arrived, hot from the broiler and brimming with big button mushrooms. They were stuffed with a rice mixture that didn't suffer the usual enervating loss of identity while smothered under a thick blanket of sauce and cheese. The flavor of fresh mushrooms came through so well that I asked the waitress for the recipe.

Like so many waitresses near the campus, this one wore shorts and looked like a first-year student from the university's art department, which was only about fifty steps away. So much of her legs were exposed that I can't remember a thing about her face. The young woman shrugged. "The recipe? Oh, no, you can't have that," she said and giggled, oblivious to my quest to overcome gastronomic ignorance through self-education.

I tried to think of a way to convince her I needed it, saying lamely, "Are you sure—*really* sure—I can't get it?"

She didn't answer at first, as if customers constantly bugged her about these sorts of things. Then she very publicly cocked her head and shifted her weight from foot to foot. I asked a couple more times before she finally decided it was only the recipe for the Mornay sauce that they didn't give out. Maybe recipes for the specialties can't be revealed, but mushrooms? Now she wasn't sure.

"I'll have the manager come talk to you." She disappeared into the kitchen.

A minute passed, and a woman with big bones and a deep tanning-booth glow appeared. "Can I help you?"

I explained my interest.

"Oh, I'm certain I can't divulge the recipe for the stuffed mushrooms, but let me go back into the kitchen to talk with the chef."

Amazing me, she returned with a copy of the master sheet for preparing the dish. I eagerly scanned it. "It's just a list of ingredients."

"The stuffed mushrooms are prepared in advance and shoved into the oven when someone orders them," she explained. "That's why we can't serve half orders. You can have the recipe. Do with it as you want."

The master sheet read:

Stuffed Mushrooms
Serves the masses

Cooked Wild Rice 8 lbs.

Cream Cheese 4 lbs.

Mornay Sauce 2 lbs.

Japanese Breadcrumbs 8 oz.

Cheddar Cheese ½ lb.

Yellow Onion 1 lb.

Celery 1 lb.

Mozzarella 1 lb.

The quantities were huge. I rapidly calculated—that many pounds of raw material would produce at least thirty dishes and serve two hundred, which would have been easier to determine if the ingredient list bothered to include the number of mushrooms required. On top of that, I assumed I would have to fly to Kyoto for a loaf of bread to make the Japanese breadcrumbs.

The manager speculated, "I think the cooked wild rice, cream cheese, breadcrumbs, celery, and onion are all squished together and made into balls. The stems are pulled out of the mushrooms, and the balls inserted in their place. The caps are then placed in a shallow dish, covered with the cheeses and sauce, and slid into the oven. At least that's what I fig-ure."

She invented most of the details. The way they make their Mornay sauce is still a mystery to me, and I can only suppose that this is the key to its tastiness. I subsequently wrote them three letters asking for clari-fication. I didn't receive a response to the first two and got an applica-tion for a marathon they sponsor after I sent the third.

Feeling a failure, I asked Lois, director of the Cooks of Crocus Hill cooking school, if she had a recipe for stuffed mushrooms that didn't require all the speculation and was already cut down to single-serving size.

Her eyes lit up. "Yes. I've got one from some old cooking teachers of mine. It has a little ketchup and a piece of bacon wrapped around the top. I think it's very good. And you won't have to worry about using it in your book because those people must all be dead by now."

Crocus Hill Stuffed Mushrooms Baked in Cream

Serves 6

- ✓ 1 pound very large uniform-size mushrooms
- ✓ ⅓ cup butter
- ✓ 1 medium onion, chopped fine
- ✓ 2¼ cups soft pulled breadcrumbs (meaning they're pulled out of a loaf of fresh bread)
- ✓ ¼ teaspoon ketchup
- ✓ 1 tablespoon lemon juice
- ✓ Strips of bacon, cut into bite-size pieces
- ✓ ½ cup light cream

Wash mushrooms. Dry well and remove and chop stems. Melt butter and cook onion. Stir in breadcrumbs and cook about 2 minutes.

Mix in lemon juice, and ketchup. Stuff mushroom caps and garnish with small strips of bacon to form a cross.

Arrange in a baking dish and pour cream around mushrooms. Bake at 400° for about 20 minutes. Serve warm, directly from baking dish.

The first time I had seen substantial mushroom expertise displayed before a public audience, I was working for the local contemporary museum, the Walker Art Center. John Cage was the visiting performer. This avant-garde—step back, please, I'm making art—musician got away with artistic murder, I thought. Nobody really seemed to understand or enthusiastically enjoy his musical creations. Still, throngs came to his performances to be able to say they saw him and to see if he'd do anything outrageous.

Cage had become such a fixture on the New York performance art scene that this trendy Midwestern museum could hardly go a year without the curators trotting him out. They did this for no other reason than to prove that, even if their bodies were in Minneapolis, damn it, they would show that their minds were still where they should be: back in Gotham.

One of my responsibilities was to drive the museum van, hauling around either art or people. On this evening, after his performance with a dance troupe, I drove Cage and members of his covey to the Tudor mansion of a major donor.

When we pulled up, Cage emerged from my van. He wore new jeans that were too large and draped over his shoes. His wispy hair stood up in a cowlick, as though he'd just rolled out of bed, making him look like the uncle a distraught family keeps in the basement. Like many celebrities who are easily recognized within their circle, Cage adopted a rehearsed expression to handle every situation. This was especially effective now, while walking amongst his fans.

To do this face, he raised his eyebrows as if surprised, opened his mouth, and stuck his tongue halfway down his chin—leaving it there like a waterslide at some abandoned motel's swimming pool. For hours I had watched him giving this look to people at the museum. Now, as he alighted from my van, he tongued, eyebrowed, and headed up the lawn.

Predictably, an adoring crowd spilled from the house to greet him with stuttering chatter and excitement—until he stopped in the middle of the lawn and started picking the mushrooms.

"Oh, these are good. Yes, these are very good," Cage said authoritatively. Eyebrows. Open mouth. Tongue. Mushrooms. Immediately the throngs fell to their dry-cleaned Ralph Lauren–clad knees, raking the turf with bejeweled fingers, hoping to turn up a single fungus to present to Cage.

"Mushrooms have always been of great interest to me. Always," he said, encouraging them. After compiling two large handfuls from the lawn and nearby shrubs, they headed inside to the kitchen. With the houseful of art museum aristocracy agog, Cage spent the next half hour sautéing the mushrooms, proving the power of mushrooms in the hands of the famous.

Wanting to know more, I asked around for a mushroom wrangler, finally discovering that a friend of mine was an expert in something besides poker. Pete Hautman—a great big guy with Buddy Holly glasses and a Buddy Holly haircut that made him look both studious and impatient—had been hunting mushrooms for years. Like me, he'd freelanced for years and was breaking into writing novels, having since succeeded. I tentatively approached Pete on the issue of morels, feeling like an idiot asking about things someone living in Minnesota ought to already know.

"You want me to take you mushroom hunting?" he volunteered over the phone.

I liked the authority in his voice. It made me forget how difficult finding morels had been portrayed. "I'm fascinated by morels."

"A lot of people are," Pete said.

"I've read reports in the paper about campers who make their own mushroom soup out in the wild—and kill themselves. I don't want to start picking mushrooms on my own and hope for the best."

"Oh, yes," he said gravely. "There are several kinds of mushrooms that will create a toxic condition in the body that can't be reversed. I know of cases where the doctors stood by and there was nothing they could do for the victim except watch him die slowly over a period of days while his body turned into a toxic waste dump." This made me wonder if I wouldn't just as soon stick to cellophane-wrapped grocery store mushrooms with perfect little caps and no taste, even if they were alleg-edly grown on horse manure.

Pete brushed off my concerns. "No, no, don't worry about picking the wrong mushroom out in the woods. Morels are an obvious type. If they're out, we'll find them. I'll point them out to you." He went on to reassure me, "I can find you some. I'll call you when it's time."

"Then we can't just go this afternoon?"

"Come on—morels? Not yet!"

I felt stupid again. "About when do they show up?"

"Mother's Day is what I usually shoot for. I've found them all the way into the first weeks of June and earlier in May. It just depends."

I prefer setting times for things, putting them on the calendar, plan-ning ahead. Pete knew mushrooms, and they couldn't be timed pre-cisely, especially not a mushroom with the stealth of the morel. I waited several days, until I got a message.

"George. It's time. Let's set up our mushroom hunt."

When I called back, Pete sounded happy, as if he'd suddenly discov-ered that a bottle of fine port had just matured. "I heard they have them in Stockholm." A small Wisconsin town on Lake Pepin, south of the Mis-sissippi River, with bluffs and trees, where his girlfriend had a cabin, seemed like the perfect breeding ground. "Watch the weather report for areas where it rains—that's where we'll go. Be ready."

He described an elaborate plan to meet me there the next Tuesday morning, but I got another call Monday night. Pete had been down to Stockholm the day before to stay at the cabin, and he checked out the surrounding area. "Too little rain down here," he said on the phone. "They only got three-eighths of an inch in the last week. Not enough moisture to bring them up. I'll come back up to the Cities in the morn-ing, and we'll go from there."

It seemed like the morels were sneaking from state to state, shifting locations at will to confuse the hunters. I imagined them stealing cars and driving back roads from one isolated location to another, or duck-ing behind trees to escape detection.

Pete pulled in front of my house midmorning in his dirty black Audi and started unpacking his trunk. "You ready?" He pulled out a wicker picnic basket, the old-fashioned kind with woven sides and a double-hinged lid. He did not look as though he'd prepared a picnic in that basket. If anything, he had brought a basket full of cigars and planned to sit on a rock in the woods, smoking them all afternoon while he watched me crawl under bushes.

"Can you drive?" he asked as he brought the basket over.

"Sure, I can do that."

"Oh, and what to wear—you're going to want to change. It's turkey season, so don't wear red, blue, or white, and don't carry a Pepsi can because it looks exactly like a turkey's head. A hunter will shoot at it. Wear long pants, sturdy shoes, and a long-sleeve shirt because we'll be walking through thorny bushes. It'll be cool, which'll be good."

He lifted a basket lid. At first all I could see was a pile of cloth bags. They'd obviously been collected over years of mushrooming and bore the labels of a variety of stores and events. One had a logo from a computer design convention. Another, a faded Pillsbury flour emblem. It all had a faint odor of earth, that rich, reeking scent that can't be described specifically but is familiar to anyone who played in mud as a child. I drew confidence from the fact he didn't carry a mushroom guidebook.

"Look at this." Pete unfolded the torn top of the weather page printed from today's newspaper. A state map surrounded by temperature listings indicated the range of the recent rainfall. It showed a dark area up north, an irregular blob that got over three inches. "You see that down at Stockholm there's not much of anything. Up here, toward Elk River, maybe thirty minutes north, there's a good chance there's enough moisture, and it's going to bring these things out. Morels need the right amount of rain, or they'll only get as big as my thumb—that's if they come up at all." Pete held up his big hands, and I realized I would settle for finding a morel the size of the last joint on his little finger.

Pounding up the interstate, Pete tutored me on mushrooming. He divulged his old family morel recipe and told me other morel stories. Those I found most fascinating were the bits and pieces sounding mythical.

"I recall the first time I went morel hunting. I was with a group of people, and we looked for hours—nothing. I thought we'd wasted the whole day. When we took a break to sit in the woods, I went to the other side of a bunch of trees, on a nature call, and walked into a big, round meadow of morels. Hundreds of them." Pete pushed his black frame glasses up his nose, using his hands to talk. "They'd been undisturbed for a long time, so they were huge. I had never seen any so big. We got bagsful, almost too much to carry. You know, it's surreal finding them like that, so many of them after looking for such a long time."

All his mushroom stories had a transcendent quality, each with a fantasy aspect and a poetic quality, putting morels in a category with Grimm's fairy tales or the witches in *Macbeth,* boiling and bubbling away at their caldrons. The secretive morel might easily be one of the ingredients in a witch's brew, or it could take witches to find one. They're even the shape of a witch's cap.

Half an hour north, Pete guided us onto a state highway, and we soon turned onto a country road with large homes and tractor dealers.

"Somewhere around here. Stop anywhere. You'll see that different sides of the road can offer different conditions."

I tucked my pants into my socks, took a collecting bag and my Swiss Army knife. As we headed into the woods, Pete instructed me not to follow him, but rather take a parallel route. We'd cover more ground that way. I took a different route, picking my own trail through thorn bushes, staying within earshot.

As we picked through the undergrowth, Pete told me about a man who lived alone in the woods down south, along the Mississippi River. "All winter he's by himself, snowed in. To survive, he picks morels in the spring and sells them to local restaurants. To cover the most ground and get the most mushrooms, he runs through the woods. He runs through them, full speed, like a high school sprinter. Everybody has special mushrooming techniques, and running is his."

I liked the image of a hermit—a bearded renegade in tattered clothes, looking shipwrecked, surviving the intense Minnesota winter in isolation—bursting out in springtime, leaves fresh on the trees, running through the forest in search of mushrooms. Another rich fantasy of the morel hunt.

We spent an hour circling through a swampy bog, cutting back and forth, searching for dead trees, which allegedly stimulate morel growth. After we picked nothing but ticks from under our shirts, we abandoned that spot and broke for lunch at a small-town bar to regroup. After a couple beers, we headed over to a neighboring hilly area near a gravel quarry. This new parcel was very dusty with huge semis roaring back and forth along the dirt road. We parked and worked through the trees, combing the side of a steep incline. There were old, rotten, mushy mushrooms from last summer. That was all. After about an hour searching, we looped back, coming out at the road that led us to the car.

Pete groaned. "Nothing. This is a bad year for morels. There's not even a hint of them. This is the worst year I've ever seen. Usually you find *something*."

"Terrible year," I said, having nothing to compare it to. "Just terrible."

"We'll try again next May."

Pete's Old Family Morels

Get a whole bunch of fresh-picked morels and clean them thoroughly. Slice them lengthwise so they're in strips like squid. Melt a fistful of fresh butter in a cast- iron skillet or similar heavy-duty pan that spreads out the heat.

Cook the morels in the butter to soften them. When they start smelling like mushrooms—that is, when they start smelling wonderful—they're done. About 5 to 10 minutes. Pepper and salt them a little, and gather everyone around the pan. Give everyone a fork and have at them.

They're also good this way on toast and in eggs. You can put them on plain pasta, and that is about all. Cooking them in the skillet over an open fire is spectacular.

Stuffed morels and morels in tomato sauce or cream sauce wastes them because it covers the flavor. Eat morels, don't goof around with them. You don't want anything on them or in them. No garlic. Nothing. If you see anybody eating them any other way, you know they're not serious about morels.

Fruiting Your Media

WAIT A WHOLE year for mushrooms? With my mushroom juices aflame, I thought if I could just talk to one more expert on mushrooms, my curiosity would be satisfied. I looked for a resource, coming up with very little, and finally called the State Agriculture Department. The person who answered used a very proper, formal tone to explain there were four places she could refer me for information about mushrooms in Minnesota:

1. The State Ag Department Marketing Department, which seemed an odd place initially as I imagined the quiet, discreet mushrooms didn't strike me as a crop in the monumental sense that horizon-to-horizon hectares of corn are a crop. Wasn't the Ag Department too busy with the big stuff?
2. The University of Minnesota Horticulture Department. They had an information hotline, but whenever I called, I felt like I got graduate student's opinions about things they had heard of but never actually seen themselves.
3. The Mushroom Society. I imagined their meetings to be populated with lopsided characters from a *Far Side* cartoon and decided to steer clear. Probably a mistake on my part as I'm sure they were a great group.
4. And as the final option, it was suggested I call Poison Control, which could point out which mushrooms to eat and which to avoid. Whenever mushrooms come up in conversation, poisoning, toxicity, and slow, self-inflicted death become the underlying tone.

I opted for contacting the State Ag Marketing Department and talked with Kevin Edberg, assistant director of marketing. His exuberant voice was filled with enthusiasm for mushrooms. I only mentioned my interest, and he tendered an avalanche of information.

"Commercial mushrooms grown in this part of the country are of three types," he said with fervent emotion, and went on to explain.

First there are shitake mushrooms, which fall into two production categories: outdoor and indoor production. There are two big flushes of production on decaying logs during the summer. Growing conditions can't be controlled, and these part-time suppliers generally sell to local markets or have accounts with local restaurants. Then there's indoor production, usually in modified buildings, renovated sheds, barns, or dairy buildings.

"These growers can fruit their media all year round," Kevin told me. "Indoors they use logs and move them around, or use sawdust or straw substrate in a container with mushroom spawn that has moved through the building in stages. The second type of cultivated mushrooms are oysters. They're big, round, flat white mushrooms. There's a producer of these near St. Joseph. This fellow's name is Kevin Doyle, and his company is Forest Mushrooms. And the third cultivated type is the button mushroom. There's a Minnesota tradition of growing these mushrooms in caves above the Mississippi River."

"I've always seen pictures of people growing mushrooms in caves."

"That's the way they used to do it," Kevin said, as if caves had been given up during the last ice age and he didn't know how I could have clung to this misconception. "These days, buttons are shipped from growers in Illinois, Michigan, and Pennsylvania. It's a very competitive market. With button mushrooms out of the East and the concentrated channels of distribution, it's tough. It's a niche of a niche market, whatever kind of mushrooms you're dealing with. Not an easy business to get into."

Deciding I best liked the idea of contacting a mushroom cultivator—someone who was fruiting his media and making it in the rugged mushroom world—I called Kevin Doyle at Forest Mushrooms and arranged a visit.

Forest Mushrooms is near St. Joseph, an hour-and-a-half drive up Interstate 94, about 75 miles north of the Twin Cities, in the middle of corn country. It is situated on the old hog farm of St. Benedict's College, a parcel running beside a two-lane state highway bordered by trees.

From the road, nothing identifies it as one of the primary mushroom cultivation sites in the upper Midwest. Doyle deliberately keeps things low key.

I parked by an unassuming building, picked my way in through a shipping room, and was directed upstairs by a woman with shoulder-blade-length black hair wearing a tie-dyed T-shirt with jeans and sandals. She was busy boxing large oysters that looked like big white circles of pancake dough. Upstairs I found the president of Forest Mushrooms seated at a government-surplus steel gray desk, a phone glued to his ear. Doyle's bushy blond beard, long blond hair thinning across the crest of his head, plus his studious glasses, would surely combine to make him look smarter the older he gets. The desktop was covered with small, square notes, pencil scribbles dancing across them. He motioned for me to sit down as he finished his phone call.

In the past, when I've been in the office of a company president who's buying and selling and trading and shipping commodities across the country, there is a hard edge to the conversation—deals are being cut. Listening to Doyle check out prices and place orders had more the feel of a scoutmaster arranging a campout, a passionately casual tone with everyone on a first-name basis. Distributors would quote him a price on some lobsters—a reddish mushroom—and he'd frankly tell them how their price compared to the other suppliers. Then he'd punch phone and chatted for a minute about the supply of chanterelles and cremini, then asked if six pounds of dried enoki could make tomorrow's 12:10 flight.

Once he hung up the phone, he continued to talk nonstop for two hours about something he knows much too much about: mushrooms.

"I always wanted to be involved with growing something. Not necessarily to be a farmer, not exactly. In fact, I first thought I wanted to have a greenhouse. Except everybody wants to run a greenhouse. People like the smell when they go into them and like the sense they're surrounded by growing things. The problem is there aren't many small greenhouse operations that survive more than a year. Big greenhouses make it, and the new greenhouse operations are, for the most part, very big, but their margins are very thin." Doyle's phone rang, and he let the machine get it. "I liked the idea of small-scale farming, but wanted a product that could command a good price, grow all year, and one where I could develop the business gradually."

He enthusiastically explained the mushroom game, pulling books off the shelf to show photos and technical illustrations of different processes. Looking out the windows, beyond the buildings, I saw a good-size house under construction. This would put Doyle, his wife, and four children on their farm. There is a long tradition of family farming, except the farms most people think about either grow crops that sprawl over the horizon and require a combine to harvest, or they're animal operations. I imagined what it must be like for the Doyle kids at school, trying to explain that daddy farmed mushrooms.

"We grow our oyster mushrooms on straw, and when we first started, we had trouble trying to figure out exactly what the right mix of straw was to make sure we could grow the same high-quality mushrooms all the time. Now we're known for our oysters. Ours have a longer shelf life than those of our competitors because of the way we raise them."

The main thing he did to add longevity to the oysters was keep a strong positive air flow in the growing room. That keeps the surfaces of the mushroom dry which doesn't allow bacteria to get a foothold. Let bacteria get going, and the surface becomes slimy, and the mushrooms start to break down.

On our way out of his office, we walked through a large space taking up most of the second floor. At the far end, a neat arrangement of bins held clear plastic bags with small handwritten tags: lobster, morel, enoki, wood ear, among others. Kevin opened a bin.

"These are dried mushrooms."

"How long will they store like this?"

"Forever, and they don't need any preservatives so long as they're kept dry."

I looked longingly at a huge bag of large, seemingly perfect morels—the mushroom I had braved ticks and thorns and a swamp going after. Here were tons of them, sitting there, taunting me.

"The mysterious morel," I said, trying to show I knew its inaccessible and exotic characteristics.

"It's just another mushroom," Kevin said as he flattened out a package of them with his hand. "This wasn't a very good year for morels around here, I understand. Actually we usually have better luck importing them from out West—Oregon and Washington. Those morels are hardier, they stand up better to storage, and supplies are generally more reliable than local sources."

"But it's the state mushroom," I said.

"Theirs are still better. This year we didn't have that consistent of a supply from the West because, from what I hear, a lot of the roads in the mountains were closed due to the fire danger, so the pickers couldn't get up there. There's a whole subculture of people who supplement their income with mushroom picking. This season we shipped in three thousand pounds of fresh morels and another two hundred pounds of dehydrated. So much of the mushroom is water that those two hundred pounds will rehydrate out to a couple thousand pounds."

"And morels can't be cultivated—is that still the case?" I asked, hoping that had changed.

"People are trying it, but they aren't getting a good, reliable product yet. Until they do, we have to rely on the hills and forests."

We headed downstairs, through the hallway that connected the new building with offices and shipping, into the restored hog barn. The first room housed a large machine the size of two compact cars stacked on top of one another. Inside, a series of metal strips on a moving chain mixed rotting straw with spawn. The spawn from which the mushrooms grow is purchased commercially and comes sterilized, sealed in plastic bags, and refrigerated. It looks like a package of mustard seeds as it's grown on millet, the round surface providing many points of inoculation.

It took me a while to keep from calling the spawn *seeds*, *spores*, or *sperm* by accident, further humiliating myself.

On one end of the machine, the mixed straw and spawn spilled into a trough, and a revolving screw moved it to a worker who filled clear plastic bags. He packed the straw down inside each bag and wired the top closed. When finished, they looked like artificial sections of the rotten tree trunks that oyster mushrooms like to grow on in the wild.

The secret to Forest Mushrooms' success, Doyle explained, was this mixing machine. He and his wife started experimenting by growing mushrooms in canning jars in the bathroom and gradually worked their way into commercial production. This went relatively smoothly until their mushrooms started failing and their partners dropped out. Fortunately, the trouble was diagnosed almost immediately: bad straw. They changed the type of straw and the way it was mixed and instantly had a bumper crop.

Doyle and his wife found the straw-mixing machine at the International Congress on the Science and Cultivation of Edible Fungi, a trade show in Germany—who said there isn't an organization for everything? "It meant taking a second mortgage out on the house and being much more selective about the straw," Doyle explained. "I found that straw's best if it's been out in the field and weathered to get the glaze off it. Then it has to have a certain pH—not too wet—decaying just enough for the oyster spawn to get its teeth into it."

Before coming up to Forest Mushrooms, I had been so agitated with the idea of growing food on horse manure that I now felt a little disappointed seeing all the straw. I was prepared for steaming brown equestrian ordure, imagining a private herd of stallions nearby to assure a steady supply. I had checked the label on some commercial button mushrooms at the grocery store, copied down the address, and wrote the Campbell's Fresh Company—an affiliate of Campbell Soup in Blandon, Pennsylvania—asking what procedure they used to grow their buttons and if they really did use horse manure.

Inquiring with a major food-products company about something as touchy as horse manure seemed like it might make them a bit edgy. However, I heard back from J.R. Reitnauer, director of marketing/operations logistics, one of these confounding hyphenated/slashed titles. He sent a very nice letter thanking me "for expressing an interest in commercial mushroom cultivation, especially Campbell's Fresh mushrooms."

In his succinct explanation of this "endeavor requiring about ninety days all told," Reitnauer explained, "We produce a growing medium through a sophisticated composting process with the primary ingredient being straw, horse manure, or hay."

Ah—it was true!

I popped the question on Doyle as we watched his decaying straw get mixed and bagged. "You don't use horse manure, do you? I mean, everybody tells me they grow mushrooms on manure."

"You need to get closer to your food, George," Doyle said coyly and went on to describe the process of mixing the kind of compost Reitnauer at Campbell's Fresh used.

Horse manure is mixed with straw and set aside to ferment. Once it's ready, it's sterilized with steam and pasteurized to kill off seeds and bugs and to rid it of any offbeat and undesirable chemical compounds including byproducts—such as ammonia. This sweet substrate is cooled, and the mushroom spawn are introduced. Once that reaches the vegetative state, peat moss and lime are spread across the top as a water reservoir.

So how is it the oyster mushroom crop needs only straw?

Doyle explained some mushrooms are primary decomposers and some secondary decomposers. The primaries will grow on fibrous media like rotting trees, while secondary decomposers need something to grow on that is already into its decay cycle. Oysters are primary decomposers and use straw. Buttons are secondary decomposers and need manure, which has already been decomposed once as it passed through the horse.

We moved into the first growing room where plastic bags filled with straw sat on the floor, waiting for the spawn to convert to their vegetative state. In here the bags gradually become filled with a white substance the color and texture of toothpaste. Then they're moved into the next room where they fruit. We opened the door, which had a very tight seal, and entered the room where the bags impersonating trees hung in rows from the ceiling, like a little forest. They looked like hundreds of plastic punching bags with narrow corridors in between. A cool breeze blew through the peculiar shapes in the yellow light.

"Got to pull the door tight—we have positive airflow to get rid of the CO_2." Doyle gave the handle an extra tug.

All things having to do with mushrooms, at every stage, have an unearthly quality about them. Pete had earlier described finding a group of morels in the woods as surreal when he happened onto them after hunting all day. Now the oyster mushrooms, which hadn't looked like much more than large sand dollars in the storage bins, were sprouting out of the slits cut in the hanging bags, like clusters of alabaster lotus leaves. Adding to this, the bags had taken the characteristics of rotten tree trunks and their rusty colors. In the dim dampness, it was the weirdest place I have ever been.

Each bag bore three waves of fruit, so some showed small growth while others displayed full-blown oyster mushrooms, the largest growing in several fingers grouped together, with one large disc and five or six successively smaller ones piled underneath.

Doyle grabbed a clump and twisted it off at the base. "This is how we harvest them, just turn and pull. We pick about two hundred pounds a day."

We doubled back and moved from the artificial forest through another airtight door and into the packing room where I had originally come in. It felt like emerging from a primeval forest.

"It used to be the East Coast growers would fly their mushrooms to California, where they would be packed in a truck with other produce being shipped to the Midwest from the valleys out there. By the time they had flown coast to coast, then been trucked to Minnesota, the mushrooms had too many miles on them and were too old. Now we can produce crops ourselves. That gets a lot more people buying mushrooms because they're fresher and there's a much better variety to choose from."

I leaned a hand on the counter by a small packing scale. "OK. About the morel—which is what got me started on this whole thing in the first place—do you have any tips for finding the mighty morel? What do I have to do to—I mean, I'm going to be a wreck if I spend all these years in Minnesota and never find one of the official state mushrooms."

"I tell you," Kevin said, looking me in the eye as if taking me into his confidence. "I pick shaggy mane and morels out in the woods because I feel confident I can identify them, but frankly there are about ten thousand varieties of fleshy fungus in Minnesota, and it's easy to make a mistake picking them out. There are lots of lookalikes, and many mushrooms are poisonous. Mushrooms are genetically geared to break down trees. The enzymes in them are a toxin that your liver will recycle over and over again until it destroys your liver and kills you. I'm not going to eat anything I find in the woods unless I'm absolutely certain of what it is, and even then I'm going to have a spore print to make sure of what I'm getting myself into."

If Kevin wasn't tromping through the woods to gather dinner, neither was I.

June

Rattlesnake Enchiladas

The announcement for the Texas dinner went like this:

Announcement
Texas Gourmet Dinner

Armadillo Appetizer: Some friends. An armadillo is enough.

First Entrée: Bjorn and Lucretia - Bar-B-Q Beef Brisket. Low-Risk Brisket

Vegetable: Some other friends - Teddy Roosevelt Beans. Bully, Bully Beans a la Roosevelt

Some Other Vegetable: Bob and Mrs. Dute—Sam's Chili. Call the gas company if there is a problem.

Second Entrée: Jay and friend - Rattlesnake Enchiladas. Don't eat breakfast this day!

Texas Squash: Sorensen and one of his friends.

Longhorn Bread: Patrick and Friend - Texas Jalape–o Corn Bread. Patrick says he'll only bring jalape–o jelly, but we'll work on him in the meantime.

Dessert: Rex and Charlene - Pecan Cake and Homemade Ice Cream sounds good.

About the wine: Don't count on it—it ain't happening. Mr. Patrick says he will compensate for the Texas theme in a sophisticated manner involving Texas beer.

And believe me, he has your best interests in mind. So, see him there.

Come at 6:00 p.m.

Longnecks! No Stubbies!

"WHAT ARE THE six flags that have flown over Texas?" Bjorn asked me during one of his harassing phone calls about planning the next gourmet dinner.

"France, Spain, Mexico, the Texas Republic, the Confederacy, and the US," I answered, having once seen them in the floor under the rotunda of the Texas state capitol building.

There had been a major-league debate over what type of cooking to try next. We very nearly called the dinner Tex-Mex, that blend of Texas and Mexican cooking with all the colors and spices and smells. Then we decided to back off and boldly go with Texas alone, leaving me to do my usual background check on the cuisine we'd selected as the next gourmet dinner theme.

Naturally, the Lone Star State does owe much to the Mexican influence and the early Native American tribes inhabiting that part of the world. The Aztecs and Mayans introduced peanuts, squash, sweet and white potatoes, tomatoes, papayas, cocoa, vanilla, avocados, beans of Herculean versatility, and chili peppers to the world. Invading Europeans ran many of these commodities on up into Texas. The Spanish, in particular, also brought to the region sheep, cattle, chickens, wheat, rice, nuts, and some new spices, and introduced missionaries who influenced adaptation of these imported ingredients into local dishes. Texas has sun-bleached beaches on the Gulf Coast and sweeping pine woodlands in the east. West Texas is all gritty deserts and craggy mountains. The Texas Gourmet Dinner sought to re-create all the parts of that foreboding landscape, strong flavors, and raucous atmosphere.

When plotting an evening in Texas, I'd hoped for a long-horned, gutsy, flea-bitten, dust-in-your-nose night of casual elegance. Since everyone deep down wants to be a Texan—at least at dinnertime—how could it fail?

The Texas Gourmet Dinner took place on the most sweltering Saturday night of the summer. Bjorn opened all the windows and doors of his house and set up fans. Everyone wore shorts and short-sleeve shirts and took off their shoes, and God bless him, Patrick showed up with two cold cases of Lone Star beer, Jay telling him, "Longnecks! No stubbies! I say, that is what I want to see—no stubbies for a hot night in Texas."

"Longnecks, no stubbies," Patrick chanted, shifting some bottles into a bucket of ice. "Come get 'em."

It was too hot to sit. Twenty-six people walked around with their Lone Stars, talking about how long it took to cook everything—the brisket in particular took a day and a half to roast. Bjorn slow-cooked it in the oven and then on a barbecue to ease in the flavor.

"That's the secret to good Texas cooking—get a good cut of meat and cook it so slowly it doesn't know what's creeping up on it," Bjorn said.

The brisket he and Lucretia prepared was extraordinarily moist and tender. Bob and Mrs. Dute cooked a squash-and-bacon dish that went over big, considering how easy it was to prepare. Calabacitas is the name of the Mexican squash their original recipe was based on. They found an acorn squash in the store and used it, with bacon, onion, garlic, canned tomatoes, and a little corn to punch up the mellow earth tones and highlight colors that a Santa Fe interior decorator would fall to her knees to duplicate.

I also decided that, as a sign of my status as novitiate master chef—a badge of honor, a rite of passage—I would develop my own chili recipe. A good chili recipe is an indispensable offensive weapon in anyone's gastronomic arsenal. I had experienced some powerfully good chili before, but hadn't explored the ingredients and didn't know much about the subtleties of making good chili. Some of the best chili I had ever eaten I found in unlikely locations such as the Hard Times Cafe in Alexandria, Virginia.

The Hard Times serves Texas, Cincinnati, and vegetarian chili. They describe the Texas as "traditional roadhouse or chili parlor style, which gained popularity during the Great Depression." It has no tomatoes and uses coarse ground chuck that has simmered at least four hours in its own juices, and can be ordered dry, medium, or wet. Their Cincinnati chili is a "fine grind of beef in a tomato base with hot and sweet spices including cinnamon." They say that this style was first created by Greek immigrants in 1922. Hard Times Cafe vegetarian chili is a "tangy soy protein with fresh vegetables." It only tastes like there is meat in it.

Many people have asked for Hard Times' recipes—including *Bon Appétit* magazine and me—but they're kept secret. They do reveal that they age the chili to enhance flavor and never cook the chili with beans. Both beans and spaghetti are strictly a garnish. They're cooked separately and combined when ordered. The meat gets the owners' personal approval before shipment to the warehouse, and the restaurants are designed without freezers because they're dedicated to making their food fresh.

Inspired by many bowls of chili, I worked on my own recipe, changing ingredients through several small batches until I was satisfied I had mastered the art form to the extent of my capabilities. I named it for my friend Patrick.

Oort Man Chili

Serves: Depends on who's doing the eating and their enthusiasm at the moment they're served, but you could take the edge off 10 people's appetite so long as it wasn't the main course—or serve 6 quite substantially.

This recipe will leave you some extra Oort Man Chili to keep in the refrigerator to eat over the next few days, which you want—nothing's better for a winter lunch break.

- ✓ 1 cup pinto beans

- ✓ ½ cup adzuki beans

- ✓ 3 1-quart bottles of Pabst Blue Ribbon. Or try Guinness Stout, or resort to water if nothing with a distinctive flavor is available to rehydrate the beans. The beans will absorb whatever you put them in to soak.

In a deep bowl, cover the pinto and adzuki beans with an inch or more of beer and soak overnight.

It takes the adzukis—which are like BBs—a full 24 hours to come to life and be ready for action. You may need to add additional beer to them as they soak up the liquid.

Food, it turns out, is improved by three things. Desserts are improved by molasses, entrées are improved by garlic, and Texas cooking is improved by bacon. These are the three unbridled truths of cooking.

- • 6 bacon strips.

Fry these in a pan separately. Cut the bacon into ½-inch pieces and set aside. Don't get the bacon too crispy. It's best when cooked slow. See if you can get some meaty pieces and don't overcook them.

- ✓ 1½ pounds of flank steak.
- ✓ 4 cups onion cut into long, thin strips that curl and look interesting.

In a sauté pan, brown the steak in olive oil along with the onion.

When the onion is translucent and the steak is browned, it's done.

Slice the steak into $1/8$-inch flat slabs by cutting it at an angle. Try cutting the steak at odd angles to add character to the chili.

Once you have the slabs cut, slice them into rectangular 1-inch or larger pieces. As you cook these, they will break apart.

Meanwhile, prepare:

- ✓ 2 minced garlic cloves. I think garlic presses are a scam, hard to clean, and you do just as well with a knife.
- ✓ ¾ cup chopped parsley
- ✓ 4 cups canned tomatoes with the juice

You will need to add fluids to the chili pot as you cook and it's best to have things that add flavor on hand. Besides the tomato juice, you can add a cup of coffee, if the leftover beer isn't enough. These add to the complexity of flavors as they add moisture.

✓ Dash of ground pepper

✓ ½ bay leaf

✓ Dash paprika

✓ Dash oregano

✓ Dash curry powder

✓ Dash ground cumin seed—this stuff has a splendid smell, but don't overdo it.

✓ Dash ground cinnamon

✓ 2 tablespoons chili powder—this gives you the fire, more for hotter

✓ Touch of cigar ash. Don't use a cheap cigar. Get good, fresh ash from a high-quality smoke, perhaps a Zino Veritas with its charred, woody flavor. Or a Santa Rosa Churchill from a smooth Honduran tobacco that doesn't so much shout it's here as gently rap on the door. Even a smuggled Montecristo No. 2—if you can get it.

Put all of this into a big pot and stir everything together as you bring it to a simmer for at least an hour, probably longer. At first it will look like a bunch of individual pieces, but stir regularly, breaking up the tomatoes.

The longer spices cook, the weaker they generally become, so taste the chili and add more if needed. Add additional beer gradually as when the chili thickens.

When you serve it, place sour cream, shredded cheese, and raw onions on top. Lots of raw onions. This vegetable was invented to be eaten on chili.

Do the dishes. Chili is generally best the second or third day, after it's had a chance to sit.

Texas food is easy to eat. It is also friendly, a breeze to fix, hardy, challenging. There is a homey quality underlying its impetuous nature. I can eat Texas every day without getting tired of it, something the more quibbling European cooking styles don't offer me.

Texas cooking also lends itself to storytelling. We were sitting around the dinner table, not too far into the Lone Star beer, when Jay started explaining one of the unorthodox fishing techniques used by Texans he'd run across during his many travels.

"Noodlin' catfish." Jay swooped the fingers of his left hand into the air as he held the table's attention. "You see, noodlin' catfish is when you're sittin' down by the river, watching the world go by, leaning back in the Texas sun, waiting for nothing much to happen."

"What's noodlin' catfish, Jay?" Charlene interrupted, leaning across the table to listen. Sweat ran off her bare shoulders in the thick heat.

"You see, you slowly let your arm sink into the water and let it dangle there until a catfish shows some interest in it. They're curious creatures, so when they eventually ease their way over to investigate, your arm starts to feel good to them. This is because you start tickling the side of the catfish, running your fingers over the fish until it starts to get comfortable with you." Jay took a thoughtful swig of his Lone Star, leaving a drop to run down his beard. "The catfish starts to like you and nuzzles up to you, and you keep noodlin' it. You keep running your fingers on the catfish and tickling his side until you can slide your fingers up to its gills and lift it right out of the water."

There are a lot of different ways to noodle catfish. There's no right or wrong way, so long as you get the fish. This was the method Jay told me about that night, and it worked for him.

"How big a fish can you get this way?" Charlene asked, amazed at the prospect.

Jay leaned back in his chair, his long, thick white hair reaching for his shoulders. "You know, that's a problem with noodlin' catfish—the big ones. I knew a guy who racked out on a rock down by the river once noodlin', and a catfish showed up. He was taking his time feeling around for it underwater when he sensed something was wrong. There was a tug on his fingers and then on his arm, and when he lifted his arm out of the water, a 200-pound catfish had it practically choked all the way down. The big fish had its lips around his elbow." Everyone groaned. "All right then, don't believe me. You'll see."

Time had come for his entrée anyway, so Jay ran to the kitchen and hurried back with a brown paper bag. "Here, don't like my catfish story? Then prepare yourself for the rattlesnake enchiladas. Everybody get ready." He hurried around the table, handing out little green bubble-wrapped snakebite kits to everyone. Each contained venom suction cups, an antiseptic vial, scalpel, tourniquet, and instructions on how to lance the bite marks. "You might need these snakebite kits—just in case the dish isn't quite done yet."

Then he brought out the rattlesnake enchiladas I had watched him prepare. I had never seen such a spectacular preparation of a crowd for a gourmet dish they were about to be served.

Rattlesnake Sour Cream Enchiladas

Serves: 6

✓ 1 pound rattlesnake meat, skinned, boned, with head and tail end removed. Reserve tail. Cut into ½-inch cubes, or 2 8-ounce cans rattlesnake, drained and cut into ½-inch cubes.

Be careful handling live rattlesnakes. In fact, don't go near live ones. If you make the effort, you can find rattlesnake at a good grocery store, or the meat counter can order it.

✓ 3½ tablespoons cooking oil

✓ 1 pint sour cream

✓ Grinding of black pepper

✓ 6 large flour tortillas

✓ Several tablespoons cooking oil

✓ 1 15-ounce can, plus 1 8-ounce can tomato sauce

✓ 1 medium onion, chopped

✓ 1 clove garlic, minced

✓ 2 teaspoons ground cumin

✓ 1 teaspoon chili powder

✓ 1 pound cheddar or Jack cheese, shredded

In a medium skillet, sauté snake meat cubes in 2 table-spoons oil until no longer translucent, about 3 minutes. Grind black pepper over to taste. Remove from pan and place in bowl. Toss with sour cream to coat well. Set aside.

In another medium skillet, sauté the onion and garlic in 2 tablespoons oil until soft. Add tomato sauce, cumin, and chili powder. Simmer until sauce begins to thicken. Set aside.

In a heavy skillet, heat ½ tablespoon oil over medium-high heat. Add tortillas one at a time. Move and twist tortilla in pan with fingers to warm and slightly brown. Flip tortilla in pan midway through the process. This should take about 30 seconds per tortilla. As each tortilla is warmed, remove, add a sprinkling of grated cheese to the flat tortilla and 2 tablespoons of snake mixture. Roll tortilla and place in a greased pan, seam side down.

When all tortillas are rolled and placed in pan, pour tomato sauce over, cover with remaining cheese, and bake in 350° oven, until sauce bubbles and cheese melts, about 10 to 15 minutes. Garnish with snake tails. Serve with snakebite kits.

If there is a rattlesnake shortage, you can substitute chicken, which would deceive your guests, or turtle meat, which is gamy and dark. Sea turtle is farm-grown on the Cayman Islands. For an odd flavor sure to confuse the most discerning palate, substitute frogs' legs or walleyed pike cheeks.

It is best to catch and skin your own snake so it's fresh, but get it any way you can. One 5- to 6-foot snake ought to do. Or two 3- to 4-foot critters.

July

Metal Fume Fever

BJORN MET ME for lunch at Snuffy's Malt Shop where they served greasy hamburgers, heaping orders of fries, and thick shakes—all foods I do not eat anymore in hopes of keeping my cholesterol down. With bebop decor, chrome-trimmed booths, and a lunch counter, it was the perfect place to discuss ways to tie the Fourth of July to the next gourmet dinner. I was feeling a new enlightenment about cooking, a confidence in my own capabilities that had come from pushing myself to try so many new techniques. I could see a dinner as a whole—something I could never do before. When Bjorn started in about the upcoming holiday, I felt for the first time that we were talking on the same gastronomic level.

"This is the one holiday that hasn't been mucked up by commercialism, at least not totally," Bjorn said as he leaned into his Snuffy burger, talking between bites. "You know, they have cards for Mother's Day and birthdays and Easter and about everything else. We're supposed to buy flowers for Secretaries Day and Thanksgiving. Some shops sell Christmas ornaments all year long. The one holiday they haven't wrecked is the Fourth."

"So, you want to wreck it?"

"No! Give me a break. I've got an idea for a one-container Fourth of July dinner."

"A gourmet dinner where we all eat out of one what? Pot? That is where I started, with the Swanson TV dinners. They're one-container meals. I don't think something like that is going to teach me anything about cooking."

"No, Sorensen—geez. I'm talking about a clambake. That's the kind of dinner you're supposed to have on the Fourth. We'll cook it at my house, then we can all go over and see the fireworks at the capitol. It'll be perfect."

I asked the Snuffy's waitress for another bottle of ketchup. "You're talking container. What kind of container are you talking about with a clambake?" The only clambake I'd been close to was as a stagehand during a college production of the musical *Carousel.*

"That's some cooking experience, working backstage in college while you heard actors sing about a clambake."

"You light a fire in the sand, wait until it gets hot, then bury the clams and lobsters and potatoes. The steam vents out of the sand. If you want to do that, I would be interested to do it and learn about it, but where are we going to get all that sand?"

Bjorn took a last bite of burger and wiped his mouth with a paper napkin. "Sorensen! We're not going to cook the clambake in sand. We're going to invite about fifty people and cook it in a trash can."

"Trash can! Have you done this before?"

"Don't worry about it, would you?"

I could never get out of Bjorn whether he had actually done a trash can clambake before or had just heard about it. Cooking in a trash can didn't seem to me all that good an idea. I imagined the metal doing something foul to the food. I recalled a news report a few years prior that told of an in-flight food manager for Japan Airlines who committed seppuku after a load of passengers ate a bad batch of sushi while flying over the Aleutians.

It's bad business to make people sick, and I wasn't fully confident that Bjorn could fake his way through this. I wanted to make sure trash can cooking wasn't going to poison anybody, especially if we were going to open this dinner up to more people than our gourmet regulars. As the coordinator of these events, I didn't want to make a mistake. News headlines: *CLAMBAKE KILLS FIFTY—ORGANIZER FLEES.*

Driven by fear, I called the University of Minnesota Extension home economist. The extension office, which began as the place farmers went seeking information on the latest agriculture research, has an alert bunch of experts who give free advice on everything.

"Just a quick question," I said when connected to the home economist on duty.

"Yes?" Her voice came back with the shading of skepticism that comes from answering doltish questions all day.

"I'm planning to prepare a clambake in a trash can. A new, clean, never-before-used trash can."

"Uh-huuuuuh..." she said, preparing to handle one more psycho.

"The trash can is made of galvanized metal. Will it be OK to cook in?"

"No! We don't recommend it!" she snapped and fell silent.

Her reaction was so concise that it took me a second to regroup. "You wouldn't recommend it? But—OK? Is there a reason? I mean, is it because the galvanized coating melts? Or is there some other factor?"

She continued her silence, the way someone stops to think out how to explain something to a young child who doesn't quite understand how things work and needs some special help. "We've heard about trash can cooking before, and we think it isn't a good idea."

I hate it when people make statements and can't back them up, so I tried to pause equally as long. "But why? And who's we?" I asked.

"If you need specifics, I'd suggest you telephone Poison Control. They would know. But I certainly can't recommend something like this. Not in a trash can!" And I could hear her thinking, *What are you? Crazy?*

So I punched in the number she gave me, and an attentive young woman answered.

"Poison Control."

"I have a nonemergency question. Is this the right number to call?"

She let her guard down. "Sure, I can answer your question, go ahead."

"Is it safe to cook a clambake in a trash can?"

"A clambake?"

"In a trash can."

From her tone of voice, it sounded as if she thought I meant I would eat the trash can too. I explained the galvanized metal cans and layering the ingredients like clams, lobsters, seaweed, and potatoes inside and lighting a fire underneath the can.

"I've heard of people doing it. I've never heard of anyone getting sick from it." A computer keyboard clicked away. "Nope, nope. Let me try another source." More clicking. "Metals. Galvanized." She put me on hold for a minute, then came back. "Well, I don't have anything on it specifically. Nothing here about cooking in trash cans or galvanized metals. There is just one thing—a type of poisoning more typical of a factory where there's welding and the unvented gases are inhaled."

"Could this affect a trash can clambake?"

Her voice dropped an octave. "It's called metal fume fever."

I had to stop and think for a minute. "Excuse me, is that the name of the disease these factory workers get?"

"Yes, metal fume fever comes from inhaling the gases of metalworking, from welding, and other processes. I have to say, there is nothing I can find about cooking in a trash can, whether that means the can doesn't reach high enough temperatures, or that fumes aren't given off—that is, they don't occur unless the metal is cut or fused." Her wheels were turning as she made a judgment. "I know people cook this way, and usually if there's a problem with something, we hear about it. When things go all right and everybody's happy, Poison Control doesn't get a call. And actually, if some people were cooking lobster during one of these clambakes, and it was coming out real well, I suppose it would be better not to tell us here because we'd want some."

"Then you think it's OK to cook in a trash can? What if we found an aluminum trash can?"

"Aluminum instead of galvanized?"

"I have aluminum cooking pots. People cook in aluminum all the time. Would that be better?"

"I really can't say. Let us know if you find out anything more about it."

The trash can sat in Bjorn's driveway with the fire on the broken concrete. The core group of gourmets attended, along with most of the alternates. Charlene showed up alone again, and we learned Rex was making an out-of-state crusade to sell soap. A relative of Bjorn's who had been living in Africa showed up with three friends. Jay brought some people from work. Patrick couldn't find a date, so he came by himself. We had a crowd of well over fifty by the time we were done. People spread out from the house and outside across the lawn, eating off paper plates.

Preparation went like this:

Trash Can Clambake

✓ Seaweed – enough for two thick layers

✓ Whole Red Potatoes – half pound per person

✓ Chicken Lobsters – one per person

✓ Chicken – one for every four people

✓ Ears of Corn – 2 or 3 per person

✓ Clams and Mussels – 10 pounds of each or more depending upon the size of your group

Putting together a clambake is a convoluted process that begins with buying a new 30-gallon steel trash can. Any good hardware store has plenty to choose from. Beware that these may leak when you heat them up, so you'll lose some water during cooking. Sometimes they'll stop leaking once they heat up. Most trash can manufacturers have not realized the inherent cooking characteristics of these products, and don't make them clambake-tight. There will be dedicated clambake-engineered trash cans available in the future, I am certain, after manufacturers read this account.

As in selecting real estate, the three primary considerations for a successful bake are location, location, location. Situate the trash can where you won't set fire to your house or ignite adjacent flammables. Bjorn determined the best place—at his house—to conduct this ritual, was in the middle of an ancient concrete driveway. It had good access to the kitchen and garden area where we would eat. In most places, even in the heart of the city, a discrete hole can be dug into the backyard lawn—it only has to be as wide as the trash can—and the fire laid there. The concrete driveway was already torn up, so starting a fire on it and having a big burned spot wouldn't matter much to its milieu.

We made three short stacks of bricks to hold the trash can over the fire, and built a fire in the middle of them. You need a good, hot fire with a lot of depth to it, which you can get from an entire ten-pound bag of charcoal or enough hardwood to burn into a white-hot mound.

We did this all this, then started packing the trash can. I'd never put much of anything into a trash can, other than, well, trash. So this was an education. The first things going into the can were four bricks. These were placed in the bottom so they'd hold a grate up inside. The bottom grate of a Weber grill fits perfectly into the bottom of most trash cans, but experiment with it before you start this process to make sure you don't get stuck with a grate that is too big.

Next Bjorn directed me to fill the bottom of the trash can with water right up to the depth of the bricks and the grate. This water's going to heat up and steam the food.

On top of the grate, we put two inches of seaweed or water-soaked corn husks. Any good fishmonger can save you seaweed from the crates lobsters are shipped in. Ask them a few days in advance to save it for you. You're going to stack up the other ingredients in layers, with wet corn husks or seaweed in between.

I felt an odd pride in having actual fresh seaweed to use, since we were maybe a thousand miles from the ocean. It added the smell of the sea.

Over the seaweed, the food starts to stack up. A whole mess of red potatoes that have been washed, go down first. One-half-pound of potatoes per person will be about right. Over this layer, goes one chicken lobster per person. Chicken lobsters are lobsters that generally weigh one and a quarter pounds or less. Next goes the actual chicken. One plucked, cleaned, and quartered chicken for every four persons. Make sure the lobsters are alive and the chickens dead.

Next, we layer two or three ears of corn for every person. The corn requires special preparation. Strip the husk and silk, but leave one layer of husk over the kernels.

On top of everything, place scrubbed and cleaned clams and mussels, ten pounds of each. Top it off with a little seaweed and put the cover on. It is ready.

Get some help from the strongest people around to lift the trash can onto the fire, which by now is amply hot, and let it cook. Once the water at the bottom starts to boil, you want to let it cook for 45 minutes. You can tell it's done when the clams open.

Get more help and use insulated gloves to lift the trash can off the fire, and remember, it's going to be blistering with steam. Stand back when the lid is pulled off to let the steam out. We managed to move the trash can with two strong people, but be careful, because there's a lot of boiling hot water inside, and dumping dinner all over the driveway looks bad to the guests if you tip if over.

The temptation is to season the clambake. We didn't add any spices. They come after the fact, along with other condiments. To complete the journey, have plenty of melted butter, salt and pepper, shrimp sauce, mustard sauce, and sour cream for the potatoes.

We added a large tossed salad and lots of cheap wine and beer, all of which seemed essential, and ate off of paper plates in the backyard.

It stayed light past nine o'clock, and we finished eating late. Just before dusk, some friend of Bjorn—a manic man wearing a long-sleeved flannel shirt, torn shorts, and shoes with no laces—showed up in a stake-side flatbed truck. He wolfed down some lobster and grabbed a plate of salad and bread. Then he wiped his hands on his shirt. "Hey, who wants to see the fireworks? There's plenty of room in the back of the truck."

He loaded it up with clam eaters and headed off to the capitol to watch the display.

As we drove along broad tree-lined Summit Avenue—a street studded with gargantuan mansions and iron streetlamps—everyone sang patriotic songs and waved the little flags Bjorn had purchased for the occasion. We shouted our enthusiasm for trash cans, clams, Uncle Sam, and the entire United States of America. As the bombs burst in air over the majestic cream-colored rotunda of the state capitol, the play of sparkling lights and percussive sound played across our ears and faces. Loudspeakers played Sousa marches full blast.

During all the noise and lights, I thought back through the past months I had devoted to learning to cook—all the people I had met, what I had learned about techniques, styles of cooking, the way I could now hold my own in the kitchen. I had learned an awful lot during my drive to make these get-togethers a success, but they were finally getting away from me. I realized how much I had learned about cooking, and this hadn't been the only thing I was after by pulling all these people together and having them show me what to do. I had changed the way I lived and related to everyone I had met. I could cook now and give advice to others. I had learned more than I thought possible in such a short time.

I knew the next of the gourmet dinners would sum up the knowledge of cooking and managing an evening of gourmets. And it would also be the last time this group would get together.

Pitching Tent in the Jam Wilderness

JEANNE YOUNG IS a friend of mine who has always been concerned about my social life. Late one evening she called unexpectedly, agitating for me to meet a woman she had just met named Susan. After some indecision, I met Susan—a Wisconsin-Norwegian—for a blind date, and I did not need to search for another gourmet-dinner date after that.

About this time a volcano in the Philippines erupted, sending a plume of ash around the world, cooling the summer. My three apricot trees responded with an explosion of fruit. It was the first time the trees had managed anything this spectacular. Every inch of branch dangled with apricots elbowing each other for space.

The apricots went neglected most of July. It was fun, though, to walk around the trees, studying the bumper crop packing the branches. Thousands of apricots, some growing in clusters of five and six, clung tight against the bark. Fortunately, the birds didn't show much interest in them, and the squirrels preferred the nearby butternuts. A chipmunk family that lived in the foundation of Eva's house ran around, picking the apricots up off the ground, but that didn't amount to much of a loss.

Susan was around all the time now. After work one afternoon, she got after me about the apricots.

"If you want to make jam, let's get on with it."

"I thought they were going to grow more. I thought apricots grew larger than this."

"You thought wrong. This is as big as they get. If you want to make jam, we're going to have to get started," she said. But how could I learn to pitch my tent in the jam wilderness without knowing more?

That evening we took another quick look through the rest of the cookbooks in my collection. *The New York Times Cookbook* side-stepped the jam issue. Other books touched on jam as novelty cooking without enough detail. Most of the recipes had cute overtones and added nuts or spices, but none provided a sweeping overview of the un-tamed jam vista. I loaded Susan into my car, and we hurried to the big Barnes & Noble that let you sit and read for hours. We could plow through everything they had on jams before closing.

The well-lighted bookstore was organized into a series of central ar-eas with tables and chairs in nooks to let you get out of the way and read. We wound around to the cooking section and found it divided into sub-categories: wok cooking, baking, organic, vegetables, "Preserves!" Su-san steered me to the thin volumes grouped together. We desperately thumbed through the twenty-five books aimed at preserves, canning, jams, and jellies from all different angles. All this information should have helped, though the more we scanned for facts, the more confusing it got.

"When does a jam stop being a jam and become a conserve? When's a preserve a curd or jump to being a chutney?" I couldn't figure it out.

Susan looked as confused as me. "The recipes for jam are all over the place in their listings of ingredients. How much fruit to sugar are you supposed to mix? How long do you cook the mixture, and when is pectin necessary and when not? No two recipes agree."

The jam experts talked in their books about a lot of fruits, though apricots were seldom mentioned. However, peaches were, and we took it on faith that these two fruits shared enough characteristics that they would react similarly when cooked. We also solved the mystery of the differences between the categories of preserves.

Jam: This uses whole fruits, slightly crushed, and evenly distributed in their own syrup. Jam can be prepared by cooking it on the stove or by storing in the freezer. It is processed with sugar and pectin. Lemon juice is often added to help set the fruit and enhance the flavor. Freezer jam doesn't get cooked but stays frozen until you need it. Jam can also be made in the microwave, but really, is nothing sacred?

Conserve: A stately fruit concoction with added nuts, cognac, dried fruit, or spices. Good for pouring over ice cream.

Jelly: This jelled juice is clear and sparkling and jiggles. The clearer, the better.

Curd: A thick, fruit-flavored combination of sugar—as you'd suspect—butter, and eggs. These are big in Britain, where orange and raspberry curds are available most anywhere.

Marmalade: Sweet jelly with citrus fruit and peel mixed in.

Butter: A luxurious intermingling of fruit pulp run through a sieve. Sugar is added, and it's cooked until it forms a paste. Spices can be added. Apple butter is an old favorite, but any fruit will work.

Chutney: Mixed fruits cooked in vinegar, sweetened with sugar, and spiced. Sauces, mustard, and other ephemera can be preserved by similar methods.

According to the many resource books, there is no limit to what can be preserved, but I didn't want to make things that nobody was going to eat. For example, if I made pickles, was I going to be able to talk any of my friends into eating them? I knew Susan and I could pound down whatever jam we made, but there was not much use to making chutney unless we could eat it. Nobody I knew would trust my chutney enough to eat it. My parents received homemade gifts for a long time, things like pickles, marmalades, and some other weird stuff. Years later, it all still sits in their kitchen cupboard untouched.

Once I started looking into the ways to prepare jam or something like it, I wondered what fruits could be used. Off the top of my head, there were apricots, mangos, grapes, plums, pears, and other fruits that could be made into preserves of different kinds. I wondered about berries. They were a natural choice for making jam. A comprehensive list of berry combinations was impossible to find, and creating one myself was not easy as there are obscure varieties out there—some robust, others not, many growable under only very specific conditions.   I checked several sources for information, including the State Arboretum Library and several berry organizations. Most didn't bother to respond with information about berries to make into jam.

The California Strawberry Advisory Board in Watsonville sent back an unsigned note saying, "We received your request for strawberry varietal information. Unfortunately, we will not be able to help you either [sic]. As a generic marketing organization, it is our policy not to discuss varieties."

Of course, this wasn't what I had asked them about, and I figured if they were going to be so careless and rude about responding to inquiries, I would never eat another strawberry in my life.

The North American Wild Blueberry Association in Canada was helpful with brochures and information, but they didn't have a comprehensive berry list. Like most organizations, they knew their niche and little about anything outside it.

Seeing a missing link in the greater berry knowledge, I compiled my own list of edible berries, wondering if one day I might try to preserve them all.

Edible Berries

The majors, such as raspberry and boysenberry, are easy to learn about. Those out of the mainstream are much harder to find. Some berries can only be eaten in small quantities or they become a cathartic—meaning a strong laxative—or they will kill you. Sort of the same thing if you ask me.

The roots and stems of otherwise edible berries can be poisonous, and some of the berries can be eaten only at certain times of the year, so ask locally and talk with an expert before eating any.

Bar: Known as the mountain grape.

Bear

Black

Blue: Big, round, used in muffins.

Boysen: Cross between logan, black, and rasp (by Rudolph Boysen, died 1923).

Bramble: Also called cane or bush, and used interchangeably with black, dew, rasp, boysen, logan, and young.

Buffalo: Native to the Far West and are edible after a long freeze.

Bunch

Checker

Choke: Unattractive name for something to eat.

Christmas: Also called toyon.

Cloud

Cran: A tradition at Thanksgiving.

Crow

Currant: A berry by any other name, comes in red, white, black, and other colors.

Dangle

Dew

Dog

Elder

Farkle

Goose

Grouse

Hack: Also called sugar, spoken of by Homer.

Hobble

Huckle: Name borrowed for a Mark Twain character. There are several varieties.

June: Commonly called service, shad, saskatoon berry, or may cherry.

Lingon: Mountain cranberry, used on Swedish pancakes

Logan: First grown by Judge James H. Logan (1841–1928). Hybrid of western dewberry and red raspberry.

Marion: A cross of the logan, black, and boysen.

Marsh

Mul

Nanny

Partridge

Pigeon: Known as pokeweed. The root is poisonous, but the early settlers apparently ate them.

Poke

Rasp: Comes in red, purple, black, and yellow.

Silver

Sloe: Found on the 53,000-year-old Ice Man in the South Tyrol.

Snow: Also called wax or Indian currant; berries remain on bushes most of the year.

Soap

Squash

Straw: Don't ask the Strawberry Advisory Board about varietals; they won't help.

Tay: Named after the longest river in Scotland.

Thimble: Light red, sweet.

Water

Whortle: A black huckle.

Wine

Worcester: Black currant crossed with goose.

Young

There are others, and I encourage you to go find them.

Having gorged ourselves on preserve information, Susan and I dallied away another week, riding bicycles into the late afternoon and getting psyched up enough to actually make some jam. When we could wait no longer because we were losing the apricot crop, we set an evening aside and headed for the kitchen. At one end of the center island sat a silver colander with a mountain of apricots freshly picked off my trees, a dozen Kerr jars, five pounds of C&H cane sugar, liquid pectin, and seven conflicting jam recipes.

"Uuuugh, I'm going to begin boiling water to sterilize the jars." Susan filled a pasta pot and submerged eight of the jars.

I scanned the recipes. "Ummmm, it says to peel peaches in all these recipes." I took a knife to the skin of one of the small, golden fruits. "Does that mean we should peel apricots too?"

"It must. If we dip them in boiling water it's supposed to make removing the skins easier, at least as far as peaches go."

We dipped a couple apricots into boiling water and proceeded to cut away the peels. While peaches are a large, easy-to-handle fruit, apricots are small and dense, so peeling them was like performing microsurgery on acorns. After peeling four with enormous difficulty, we caved and left the skins on. We just cut them in half and pried out the pits.

Once the fruit was ready, we looked over the recipes again, trying to find some common instructions running through them. We tried this and that, never understood why lemon juice was necessary, and refused to believe that so damn much sugar was truly needed—most recipes called for twice the amount of sugar as fruit. Cooking times were all over the place—fast, slow—with instructions to add ingredients in different orders. We speculated about how long to boil the jars and lids to kill the bacteria, and finally just did everything at once. We mixed sugar into the fruit in a pot, and when I turned my back, it boiled over, pouring a sea of gummy lava over the gas flame, snuffing it out. We quickly changed burners, but because we'd dumped too much sugar into the pot and cooked it too long, there was too much liquid and not enough fruit.

Susan and I stopped in the middle of all this. Every surface, every inch of counter space, was covered with drips and goops. Apricot pits skittered across the sticky floor. Recipe books with marks and spots lay all about, held open with wooden spoons. Measuring cups looked like they would never come clean. The pot with the jars boiled up, sending a plume of steam into the air. The stove could have taken a nuclear blast and not looked any worse.

"Ready to fill the jars," I said.

"Aye, aye, captain," Susan said, saluting with a pair of tongs.

We dove into the sealing process—all of it awkward—sliding hot lids over the tops of sticky jars, dripping apricot sugar on the floor, stepping in it, tracking goop around.

"Over here." "Once more." "Almost full." "A little less syrup." We barked orders at each other as we lurched through the unfamiliar routine.

Hours later we sealed the last jar, then boiled them all again briefly to assure the seal and integrity of the ingredients. The finished jars, lined up on towels in neat rows, retained their heat for hours, feeling like little radiators. They weren't completely cool until they had sat overnight.

The next morning I wiped the outsides of the jars clean, then made and attached labels which read:

Suzy's Wicked Jam
Apricot Confusion
Organic—Home Grown

August

Oort Man the Greek

WHILE HANGING AROUND Jay's duplex out on the porch, we kicked around several suggestions for what region to spotlight for August, talking it out over a bowl of tortilla chips and a jar of Paul Newman salsa. Jay suggested we take another look at the planet. His atlas appeared, and in the harsh midsummer light pouring in the windows, we scanned the hemispheres and the continents.

"Down here in Africa?" Jay let his fingers travel across the page. "Jungle food? No. Australian? No. We'd never get the ingredients—whatever they are. Malaysia, Borneo, Nepal, any of these out-of-the-way places are going to be tough." He sat back in his chair, trying to relax his way into a suggestion.

I couldn't come up with anything. Though, I had decided this would be the grand finale, and wanted to make it memorable. Jay brought one of his pipes. He took a lot of time tamping the tobacco into the bowl and firing it. After a few puffs, he tipped his head, running a hand over his beard as something occurred to him.

"This is going to be the big sendoff dinner?"

"The final hurrah." I nodded.

A light glint in his eyes. "Toga party."

"Excuse me?"

"You want to send this off right, do a toga party. Like John Belushi in *Animal House*. Belushi looked like he was having a pretty good time in that movie."

"Yeah, Greek food," I said. "I love ouzo, leg of lamb, goat cheese."

"Toga parties—are they strictly Greek?" Jay tamped his tobacco. "I thought the *Animal House* toga party was more of a Roman thing."

"Where'd I get Greek out of that?"

Jay scrounged a couple worn reference books off his shelf and flopped them open in his lap. "Togas are Roman! The Greeks wore tunics. You want to be authentic? We'll have to make it a tunic party, unless you want to do Roman food."

"A Greek tunic party. I suppose most people don't know the difference between tunics and togas, so we'll have to make a point of educating them. This'll be a good way to end the gourmet dinners." I agreed, and it was done.

Announcement
An Evening in Ancient Greece
Tunic Party

You must wear a tunic or you can't come and that is all there is to it.

Saturday, August 8

Jay Berne will arrive at 6:00 p.m. like everybody else.

Greek food. Call immediately and tell your host what you will be bringing. This is your responsibility.

And for the first time, everyone may bring their own Greek beverage. Yes. Bring your own Greek beverage or something to share.

And remember, you must not wear a toga, toga, toga, toga, toga—

Wear a tunic, tunic, tunic!

GREEK GREEK GREEK GREEK GREEK GREEK

If it's not gourmet, it's not a Sorensen Gourmet Dinner!

End of the season - Greek - Respond immediately to reserve your place at the tunic table.

I visited Greece once in August. It's the hottest place I've ever been, beating out both Delhi, India, and Death Valley. The air was so dense with heat that at midnight, in a café tucked into the pink-sand beaches of Corfu, I couldn't sit within thirty feet of a bare light bulb because of the additional fire it radiated.

Greece was not what I expected. I wanted to step into the classical epoch with white stone-pillared buildings and people who look like the figures on ancient vases in museums. Instead I got a cluttered urban jungle. Concrete Athens was smoggier than LA. Traffic clogged the roadways. Many of the monuments had been rotted by the chemicals in the air. Nobody spouted philosophy, and it looked more like Mexico than anywhere else I had been. What had happened to this place? Where were the Greeks I'd heard so much about over all these years? Had they all moved away?

I decided not to try to re-create contemporary Greece for one dinner. Instead, I would go for re-creating a fantasy night in ancient Athens, sending my gourmet cooking teachers off with an evening they would remember.

There was a lot to build the evening on, since Greek cooking demonstrates a direct lineage to 900 B.C. At that time, Greece began a 700–year reign as a powerful military force in the Mediterranean, with colonies spanning all the way to Persia and India.

By the fifth century B.C., Greeks could bake all sorts of breads, pancakes, sourdough, and cakes, which were offered as prizes for athletes and presented at events such as weddings. The Romans came to power in the area after 158 B.C. and held it—getting mixed reviews—until Christian Romans and Greeks overpowered them in 312 A.D. This moved the center of power to Constantinople, which became the largest city in the world for a millennium and created the age of the Byzantines. No good food must have come from it since you never hear of a good Byzantine restaurant.

Things have gone back and forth in Greece ever since, mixing up the menu. The crusaders trudged through the area, changing it further. Marco Polo introduced pasta from the Far East, while the Arabs brought eggplant, resulting in moussaka. The Byzantines folded in 1453, when Constantinople fell to the Moslem Ottoman Turks.

Turmoil of different sorts continued until the Turks were pushed out of Greece in 1821, leaving behind a further altered type of cuisine. The tomato showed up from South America at some point and is incorporated in Greek recipes routinely now. Both the British and the French spent some time in the neighborhood, and during this colonial period, upscale Greek restaurants actually listed their dishes by French names to appear more sophisticated. American tourists came in droves after fighting to keep the Nazis out during WWII, while all along the way, Greek cooking kept its integrity, adding new techniques and ingredients, changing while remaining definably Greek.

My first and strongest impression of the Greek approach to eating came from the movie *Zorba the Greek*—Anthony Quinn dancing, drinking, snapping his fingers, fooling around, dancing, fooling around some more. This type of evening would be perfect for the last gourmet dinner, so long as I could combine it with the trappings of the ancients.

After a year as an apprentice gourmet, I wanted everybody to have a good Zorba sendoff. I took it as a good sign that on the appointed evening, everybody showed up wearing some kind of tunic. Some people sacrificed old sheets and draped them over their shoulders. Others made elaborate robe-work out of fabric, with cords around their waists and an extra length of cloth draped over one arm. I spent two hours on a borrowed sewing machine shaping my own costume. I attached stars and moons on the front to give it a half-Greek, half-wizard look.

The grapes I had planted two years prior augmented the costumes. They had grown into miles of vines, covering a heavy trellis beside my deck, and were bearing small clusters of fruit. As each guest arrived, I cut several feet of vine and helped wrap it around each person's head, careful to arrange a bunch of scrawny grapes to dangle over their eyebrows.

A friend of Lucretia's—trying for maximum Greekness—even pinned a paper-letter acronym to the bosom of her tunic: AGN. Everyone finally figured out it sounded out to say "Aegean."

The tunics made a huge difference in pumping up the atmosphere at the gathering. So did the vigorous smells that filled the house and spilled out onto the deck as the food passed through the final stages of preparation in the kitchen.

One couple who had never come to one of these before, arrived in full-blown tunics made with the wife's substantial costume shop skills. They looked terrific, but the two could only stay a short time before heading downtown to a formal banquet. When it was time to go, rather than change, they went directly there, wearing their robes with grapevines around their heads. I wished I could have watched their entrance at that stuffy downtown St. Paul gala.

To further enhance the physical environment and classical nature of the evening, I constructed a replica of the Parthenon in my backyard. This facade stood twelve feet tall and stretched fourteen feet across in one magnificent edifice. I used pine 1-by-3s for the frame and nailed cardboard pillars on the front, with the large peaked roof detailed in painted black lines. The nicks and curves and grooves in the pillars and cornices loosely interpreted the original design. I wrote across the top: *An Evening in Ancient Greece* with some bogus Greek alphabet characters for style points.

Jay's brother Chris, who I had traveled with, arrived in the heavy folds of a tunic with a turquoise sash and low-top hiking boots. He carried an ovenproof dish covered with aluminum foil. He peeled the cover back, revealing a jumble of dark shapes drenched in a thick soup.

"Octopus!" Chris proudly puffed his chest.

"Octopus?"

"I did it all myself."

"You bought a whole octopus?"

"A whole fresh octopus."

I hadn't realized his enthusiasm for getting down to cooking basics, much less tackling something this gastronomically aggressive. He explained how he skinned the entire octopus by first cutting the skin at the head, then rolling it down each tentacle.

"It rolls down like a sock. Like this—" He lifted his leg, pulled up the hem on his tunic, and rolled down his gray-flecked wool sock. "You just start rolling them down, and the farther you go, the more white meat you see, until you have the octopus sort of inside out. It took me nearly two hours to unroll him this time, but then, I had never rolled the skin off an octopus before. I'll be a lot faster next time."

Jay looked equally ancient and funky in the tunic he'd made for himself out of castoff camping supplies. His white beard and hair made him look a little like Father Time. He'd gotten heavily into research on the Greeks and developed a stuffed grape leaf recipe that people loved.

Stuffed Greek Grape Leaves in a Yogurt-Mint Tunic Sauce

Serves 4

Make the Tunic Sauce

- ✓ 1 cup plain yogurt
- ✓ ½ of a fresh cucumber, grated
- ✓ 2 tablespoons onion, finely chopped
- ✓ 2 tablespoons lemon juice
- ✓ 4 tablespoons fresh mint leaves, finely chopped
- ✓ ¼ teaspoon garlic powder

Prepare sauce by placing yogurt into bowl. Peel and grate the cucumber, being careful not to grate the seed core. Pat cucumber gratings in paper towels to remove excess moisture. Add grated cucumber, chopped onion, lemon juice, chopped mint leaves, and garlic powder to yogurt and mix well. This should be done several hours ahead of time so it has time to mellow. Stir again before serving.

Make the Stuffed Grape Leaves

- ✓ 24 grape leaves, brine-packed
- ✓ 1 pound ground lamb
- ✓ ¼ cup onion, finely chopped
- ✓ 3 tablespoons olive oil

- ✓ 3 cloves garlic, minced
- ✓ 1 tablespoon leaf oregano
- ✓ Black pepper
- ✓ 2 tablespoons pine nuts, minced
- ✓ 2 tablespoons tomato paste
- ✓ 2 cups white rice, cooked in chicken broth
- ✓ 1 tablespoon vegetable oil
- ✓ 1 small can olives

Preheat oven to 350°. Drain and separate grape leaves and place them in a pot a few at a time. Boil for 30 seconds. Remove and allow to dry on paper towels.

Sauté ground lamb in 2 tablespoons of olive oil for 5 minutes. Add chopped onion, garlic, and oregano, and cook for another 5 minutes, until lamb is no longer pink. Add a sprinkle of salt and generous grinding of pepper.

Cook rice in chicken broth. Put cooked rice in mixing bowl and add lamb-onion mixture. Add tomato paste, 1 tablespoon olive oil, black olives, and pine nuts. Mix in bowl to blend all ingredients. Mixture should hold together but not be wet.

Place grape leaves two at a time on work surface, overlapping one-half of each leaf. Mound 2 tablespoons of rice-lamb mixture on each pair of grape leaves. Roll leaves around rice mixture, packing tight, folding in outside edges to form a closed package. Repeat for 12 filled rolls.

In an oiled 9-x-13 glass baking dish, place rolls seam side down. Add 3 tablespoons water and cover dish tightly with foil. Place in oven and cook for 15 minutes, or until heated through. Transfer to serving dish and top with Tunic Sauce.

More than thirty people showed up for the wonderful food-laden atmosphere, dancing in their tunics, filling plates with a range of Greek delicacies. I really did feel Greek cooking was a fitting end to the gourmet dinners. We'd covered many themes and tackled some of the world's best cooking. I had learned a great deal about entertaining too. For one thing, throwing a party is like directing a play. You can pick the actors and give them scenery and a script, but no matter what you do, in the end, they're going to bring their own interpretation to the parts. In the same way, all a gourmet-dinner organizer can do is give his players a place to eat and hand them a copy of the menu.

Jamming

SUSAN AND I started paying an enormous amount of attention to the jam sold in stores. Whenever we got near a grocery or a gourmet specialty store, we'd make a beeline for the preserves, examine the color, look for bubbles, check the ingredients, types of berries, where they were produced, whether or not they used additives such as lemon juice, butter, or other things. We speculated about how they cut the amount of sugar and whether it would affect the taste. We would compare our apricot jam to those on the shelves.

"Looks too jelled, like a rock. Our apricot has a more golden color than theirs." I liked to compare everything to our own Apricot Confusion. We'd been planning to make a second batch as well as some other flavors after devastating the kitchen with our first try.

About this time, the last flush of Susan's mom's raspberry crop came in down in La Crosse, and the remaining apricots were coming of age on the tree in the front yard. Some enormous peaches arrived at Lund's grocery from Colorado and Washington, and we started to see signs for the Minnesota State Fair on billboards around town. The conversation shifted from if we'd make jam again to when we'd make more, and what different types they would be.

The thin Lund's home economist, who had been one of our sources of information before, was skulking around the fruits and vegetables when I swung by for more supplies. She didn't recognize me right away, so I reminded her who I was.

"We followed your advice and made apricot jam."

"Apricots don't grow here in Minnesota," she insisted during our first visit.

"Yes, they do." She didn't remember me after all.

"Apricots—you're sure?"

"You helped me with the jars and pectin a couple weeks ago."

"Good. I'm glad everything turned out all right. What can I help you with today?"

"Which of these peaches would make better jam?"

She reached over the counter into the bin of Colorado peaches and picked one out. She rinsed it in the sink in a fruit-prep area and cut me a slice. "The only way to tell is to taste." The Colorado peach was smaller than the luscious Washington variety. It was overripe and starting to soften, though the taste was good. Next she selected and sliced a Washington peach, which was firmer, less ripe, with a robust taste.

"That's the one." I picked out ten pounds of the best Washington peaches.

Now we had fresh peaches, organic homegrown raspberries, organic homegrown apricots, and tons more jars, pectin, sugar, and lemon juice. We had decided that adding lemon juice, which some of the recipes had called for, brings out the flavor and, I suspected, enriches the color.

Susan and I pulled together all the components and prepared my kitchen for a major jam-making weekend. We brought out the utensils, wooden spoons, jar funnel, lids, jars, measuring cups, special tongs with a wide grasp that can pick up jars by their side or top. I created a water bath in my largest pasta pot for sterilizing the jars and gathered sugar, pectin, fruit, and lots of towels for the expected mess.

We cranked up the stereo and started making raspberry jam straight from the Certo pectin recipe. It turned out too stiffly jelled. That didn't stop us. We switched to apricot-raspberry, creating two different batches from three recipes. Into four jars of the apricot-raspberry, we added cognac from airline liquor miniatures and designated these a conserve for ice cream.

For peach jam, we picked a recipe from a book on preserves, took a chance, and doubled the amount of peaches it called for in order to reduce the sugar. As the peaches cooked, it was difficult to crush them, and we ended up smashing them with a whisk so they broke into unequal-size pieces. Some were too big, and others smashed to pulp. Next time we'd cut them smaller before tossing them into the pot. We made apricot jam again too, this time with more confidence, since Apricot Confusion came out so well.

On Monday I called the Creative Activities Department at the Minnesota State Fair and explained that we were entertaining the idea of entering our jam. They sent a guide to entering the competitions they hold in a broad range of categories. The fair puts up $10,000, which is divided among the many winners. In most disciplines, the prizes run from a top of $6, to $4, to $2, down to only a ribbon for fourth place. Homemade items can be submitted across all frontiers. There are table linen competitions, crochet and knitting, every kind of baked product, needlecraft, weaving, and even knotting, felting, and canning. For woodworkers there is canoe building, dollhouse construction, and whittling. There are a few special rules and restrictions, as the entry form says: "No cans, wedding gowns, or baptismal gowns will be accepted in any category."

Our interest was preserved foods, which the little yellow folder showed was divided into jellies, jams, butters, pickles, and canned vegetables. Susan and I imagined ranks of little old ladies, kettles steaming on their stoves across Minnesota, with monster baskets of colorful fruits and berries oozing juice, all competing for the prestige of beating out other little old ladies for the best jam. Stories abounded about competitors who entered dozens of categories each year at the fair, trying for ribbons, scrambling over each other for the top prize.

All our jams sat for a week, carefully lined up on the kitchen island for a close examination so we could selected the apricot, peach, apricot-raspberry, and raspberry from the lot. I held them up to the light to check the color and hunt down bubbles, crystals, missed pits, stems, leaves, and lord knows what else. If you're going to enter a competition, you want to pick your best jar of jam. Some jars did look better than others.

The peach jam appeared absolutely radiant; it practically glowed. The apricot appeared more honey-colored, with small, evenly sized pieces of fruit distributed uniformly throughout. I wished the apricot glowed more, like the peach, but the nature of the fruit was different, so I selected the best one and moved on. The raspberry all looked the same. The seeds were spread nicely around the glass, and the ruby fruit showed profound depth. Raspberries are common in this part of the country, so I expected the raspberry competition to be the fiercest. The apricot-raspberry jam was runny—no surprise—it had been an ad-libbed concoction. We had experimented by not using pectin in this batch and cutting back the sugar on the theory that the density of the fruit would keep it thick. It didn't work.

I spent most of the next afternoon making labels. The preprinted jam-jar labels available in hardware stores were little ovals with bright red and blue flowers printed across the top and black lines to write the name of the contents on. Sealing, label, and container counted for 10 percent of the score, leaving me hoping that if I did my own, the judges would applaud the extra effort. I cut down four of my self-sticking address labels, removing my name and address and the yellow palm tree I use as my logo. The resulting rectangle was large—at least double the size of the little ovals—and I wondered if it would block the view of the jam inside.

What the hell—I tested three pens to make sure they were waterproof and lettered *Suzy's Wicked Jam* with the name of the flavor underneath and, in the case of apricot and raspberry, wrote that it was organic and homegrown. I drew little pictures of apricots and raspberries and peaches on the appropriate labels above the name of the fruit and colored them with fluorescent highlighters. The labels looked like a kid had done them during recess, but they had an honest quality—a *je ne sais quoi* I was sure the competition would lack.

The next day, the uniformed police officer at the entrance to the fairgrounds motioned for me to stop.

"Creative Activities?"

"Oh, yeah."

He smiled, knowing I probably had a trunk load of homemade birdhouses. "That yellow building over there."

The large wooden structure had four sets of doors open across the front with a line of folding tables studded with neat and clean ladies— all with white hair—every one of them smiling, greeting the stream of contestants who arrived with bags and boxes. I approached two petite women who could have been my lunatic grandmothers.

"Hello," I said.

"Hello," they answered.

"Have you made a previous entry this year?" the one on the left asked. Pulling forward a multiple-copy form, she began to fill it out.

"No, this is my first entry," I said proudly.

"Oh, good. And what are you entering?"

"Jam."

She stopped writing. The pen fell out of her hand. "Oh, what kind? I love jam."

"Maybe we'll eat it all ourselves," the woman beside her said, reaching for my bag.

"What kind?" the first one asked again.

"Yes, what kind do you have?" the second demanded.

"Four kinds." I set the jars on the tabletop, thinking they might really eat them. "Raspberry, peach, raspberry-apricot, and apricot."

"Oh, that's wonderful," the lady filling out a yellow form said. "Wherever do you get apricots?"

"I grew them."

"You grew apricots!" the two said in unison, amazed. "No. That's impossible. You can't grow apricots in Minnesota."

It felt odd leaving little jars of jam at the fair. Knowing the popularity of the competition, they would be a few among thousands of entries. As I left, I looked around, trying to catch a glimpse of a granny with a more translucent jam, a more fluorescent label, fewer crystals, better color—hiding it under her shawl while sneaking up to the table, sliding her jar over the transom, harboring a secret recipe, slithering through all the forms, knowing she was going to blow through the judging with decades of expertise, years of enduring steaming stove vapors, finding the most luscious fruit, surviving one competition after another.

We waited a week until opening day, then, dressed in shorts and aloha shirts, made a pilgrimage to the fairgrounds. The largest crowd for an opening day to date crammed into the site of the Great Minnesota Get-Together. We cut across the deafening midway, which seethed with chubby young men in dirty T-shirts hawking stuffed animals. Strolling farther into the fairgrounds, we saw the grandstand housing an endless variety of tacky products—vibrating pillows and vegetable choppers sold by hucksters wearing microphones around their necks. Throngs stood in long lines for pronto pups and breaded cheese curds to be washed down with Pig's Eye beer. At the far end of the fair, Machinery Hill displayed tractors, dicers, and other odd, dangerous-looking farm equipment.

Susan and I strolled through the honey competition, the sunflower exhibit, forest ranger fire tower, live trout ponds, French fry booths, mini donut vendors, and politicians. The Republicans had a stuffy little booth resembling a prison cell. The Democrats, archaically the Democrat-Farmer-Labor party, had a larger, happier display.

Our anticipation heightened as we entered the banana-colored Creative Activities building. The crowded space inside was packed with display racks of quilts and large glass booths full of handmade furniture. Wooden ships under full sail vied for attention with stamp collections. Where else could anyone hope to display some of those things?

We dodged around a group of plaid-wearing women in rocking chairs, who were conducting a knitting bee that made knitting seem even more tedious than it probably is, and headed for the foods. In tall display cases sat breads cut into slices with the loaves behind them. Jellies were backlit in a glass display, giving the jars the look of taillights leaving a parking lot.

"Jams? Know where they are?" I asked so anyone within range might respond.

"Over that way," a man in overalls said as he tugged at his wife's large forearm. "That's them, ain't it?"

Pies filled the bottom of the cabinet, and above them, five glass shelves held an army of jars that seemed divided into categories. The raspberries were easy to spot because of their color and seeds, but all the labels were turned away, showing only the backs. There were no signs indicating the type of jam on any shelf or who submitted it.

"That must be blackberry. You can't tell for sure." Susan tried to guess the types of jams from their colors. The first four finishers in each category were positioned in a row with the ribbons indicating first, second, third, and fourth. The rest of the jams in the running were spaced out across the shelf so one type of jam dissolved into the group of jars of the next.

"There!" She pointed at a jar she could see the side of. "Didn't you say you made big labels? That one's got a big label! A really big label! Doesn't that look like...like—"

"Apricot," I said.

The edge of the label on one jar was visible. It looked like my hand-drawn art. A string was taped to the top, and a blue ribbon hung down the back of the jar.

We didn't even place with our other three jams. Yet, on the first try, I saw that my year of gastronomic hardship had paid off, and I had the evidence I needed to prove I had really become a gourmet.

We'd won the blue ribbon for apricot jam at the Minnesota State Fair. In the Midwest, there is no higher recognition for being a gourmet. The jam scorecard read nearly perfect marks:

MINNESOTA STATE FAIR
Score Card
CONSERVES AND JAMS
Lot No. 491 Entry No. 13

Possible Points, Our Score

General Appearance: Sealing, label, container; lid clean, tight, free from tarnish: 10, 10

Color: (natural as determined by fruit used, color deepened by right use of sugar and not darkened by overcooking): 15, 14

Absence of Crystals: 10, 10

Texture: Not too thick; should cut easily with spoon or knife. Should not be sticky, tough, syrupy, or sugary: 30, 29

Flavor: Pleasing, natural, fruity flavor, neither too sour nor over-sweet, not scorched or caramelized: 35, 34

Total: 100, 97

After Dinner

AFTER DECADES OF staring into the refrigerator, I had learned to cook a range of styles in twelve short months with the help of good friends. I had suffered much hardship along the way, learned more than I ever imagined, and discovered how much everything I did related to food. Highlights of the experience included pork roast changed into wild boar, seafood lasagna hidden on the Oregon coast, the hermit running through the woods after morels, Poison Control checking on trash can cooking, geese marching across the kitchen at midnight, and many others.

The group has not gathered since the Greek tunic party. I still see some of the people. Others have moved or otherwise disappeared.

Soon after the dinners ended, I took a break from drinking any alcohol for eighteen months. What an eye-opener. I never realized how often I was offered a drink until I started to turn them down. I experimented with fruit juices, flavored waters, and other beverages to go with meals and found they work quite well. Eventually I started sipping wine again with dinner and gradually added better wine in modest amounts. It is truly more satisfying to nurse a single glass of a great, pricey merlot than to swig half a bottle of a troublesome house red.

There has been much more jam on the program for Susan and me. Visiting Pike Street Market in Seattle, we breezed through the well-stocked Sur La Table and came out with a stainless-steel jam funnel costing fourteen bucks. If investing in an expensive jam funnel does not say a relationship will last, what does? Susan gradually revealed herself as more Norwegian than I first believed. She still salts most things and uses the recipes on pumpkin pie-filling cans and Crisco tubs, but we're working on that.

We are quite married now, with a charming boy and girl, who grew up determined to teach us an entirely new set of dining routines.

These days we invite people over to eat so they'll arrive halfway through the dinner preparations. The guests instinctively hang around the kitchen to watch and help. Long ago we learned that when friends become vested in the cooking process, they enjoy the evening far more. One of the best parts is that it leaves us all feeling we are authentic amateur gourmets.

Acknowledgments

MANY THANKS TO Susan and our overachieving children Kenzy and Bennett. Editors and advisors accomplished author Lynn Hightower, Katherine Flitsch, and Kim Robinson at Misty City Editing. Wesley Trooper, a particularly great Norwich Terrier, Brett Hall-Jones and the Community of Writers at Olympic Valley, and the UCLAx Writing Program. Stalwart friends Chris Berne, George Soule and Lisa, Cyndy Altman, Helen Petrovitch, Paul Bogden, and all the wonderful people who let me couch surf—you make travel affordable and fun. Much appreciation to Bill Burleson and the enlightened staff of Flexible Press. Plus all of you who taught me to cook.

About the Author

GEORGE SORENSEN HAS written books about writing and a history of an army unit in Montana who tried to replace the horse with the bicycle, titled: *Iron Riders*. For years he wrote marketing communications and documentation for 3M, Nike, Boeing, and other companies. He helped launch new products to market, including PostIt Notes, and worked with NASA on the Mars Program. Now he writes novels and nonfiction books—keep an eye out for them. George lives in the Pacific Northwest.

georgesorensen.com

www.ingramcontent.com/pod-product-compliance
Lightning Source LLC
Chambersburg PA
CBHW071153130626
46553CB00004B/1645